Copyright © 2025
BY: **C. Grooms & Bobby May**
All rights reserved.

No part of this publication may be reproduced, stored in a retrieval system, or transmitted in any form or by any means which includes electronic, mechanical, photocopying, recording, or otherwise without the prior written permission of the publisher and authors, except in the case of brief quotations embodied in critical articles or reviews.

For information or permissions, contact:
Ten G Publishing
New York, New York

This is a nonfiction work. All facts and events are presented accurately to the best of the authors' knowledge.

ISBN: 978-1-7359172-3-8
First Edition
Printed in the United States of America

FOR THE LOVE OF THE GAME

CONTENTS

Harlem Heat	5
Echoes of Camden	8
Canton's Calling	11
Harmony in Atlanta	14
Courtside Connections	18
Rising Stars	24
College Bound	27
Shattered Dreams	33
Brotherhood Tested	37
Courtside Ambitions	43
The Business of Basketball 101	50
Off Court Challenges	64
Harmonies & Heartbreaks	76
New Beginnings & Bittersweet Endings	86
Love, Loyalty, & Last Chances	99
Decisions & Departure	111
Rainy Days	124
Mass Appeal	131
Crossroads & Consequences	138
One Mic	144
Balancing Acts	150
The Final Countdown	157
The Echoes of Glory	162
The Road Ahead	169
The Paths We Choose	185
Family & Loyalty	196
Survival of The Fittest	208
Reflections	214
About The Authors	219
Acknowledgements	221

C. GROOMS & BOBBY MAY

FOR THE LOVE OF THE GAME

C. GROOMS & BOBBY MAY

Chapter 1: Harlem Heat

The sun was pounding Rucker Park, and the asphalt was a shimmering mirage. Malik Wright's sneakers squeaked as he faced his man, the noise of the crowd muffled in his ears. He burst past his defender, his lean frame moving faster than you thought possible. The ball was an extension of his arm as he went up for the hoop. The net swished and the bench erupted.

As Malik landed, he looked up and Jaden's voice was clear above the noise. "Malik! You're not just playing the game; you're out here composing symphonies!"

Malik smiled slightly and wiped the sweat from his brow. "It's not about music, J. It's about writing our own story."

The words hung there between them. In

Harlem, basketball wasn't just a game. It was a language, a means of expression, a way to rewrite the script society had given them.

FOR THE LOVE OF THE GAME

As the sun went down, Malik walked home the bounce of the ball in time with the city. He walked into the modest apartment he shared with his family and was immediately hit with the beats coming from his little brother's room.

Masterson was 16 and already making noise in the music scene. His group, PHP, was more than just another hip-hop group, it was a movement, and their rhymes spoke for their generation.

"A yo Mass," Malik said, pushing open the door to his brother's studio. He stopped, tilted his head to the side, and bobbed to the beat. "That's fire!"

Masterson looked up from his board, a smile spreading across his face. "Just wait, bro. This is going to put us on the map. We got a show at the Apollo next month."

Malik's eyes went wide. "The Apollo? That's big, Mass!"

Their moment of excitement was interrupted by the tired shuffle of their father's feet. He walked in the apartment, the weight of a long day's work in every step. Their mother followed behind him, her strength shining through her fatigue.

At dinner, the conversation flowed from Malik's basketball to Masterson's music to their parents' long hours to the problems of their community. The table was small, the portions meager, but the love and determination in the room was unlimited.

Later that night as the city quieted down, Malik lay in bed, his mind racing. Although it may have been for many of his peers, basketball wasn't just his ticket out of the hood, it was his essence. Each time Malik played, it was an otherworldly experience. Only a select few understood how he felt serenity even playing against the most aggressive opponents. He smiled with each foul that the refs overlooked and was sent straight to glory with each dunk. Every dribble echoed with defiance, each shot painted his fate with bold strokes, and every sprint shattered the boundaries imposed by others, as Malik was at the helm of his own destiny.

FOR THE LOVE OF THE GAME

Chapter 2: Echoes of Camden

The bounce of the ball cut through the silence of Camden's twilight. Elijah Williamson glided across the cracked court, each dribble a noncompliant shout against the urban blight surrounding him.

Elijah spun and dunked, and his friend Marcus whistled low. "Damn E. You're going hard out here."

Elijah landed soft and flashed a quick grin at his friend. "You already know!" he bellowed in between breaths, while maintaining his focus. His response was short, but his friend knew he had more to say because he always did. His mind echoed, "In Camden everything's a fight, Marcus. I'm just fighting mine with a ball instead of a gun."

Their conversation was interrupted by the inauspicious arrival of Darius, a local drug peddler, and his crew. The tension was obvious, and it cut through an otherwise calm mood.

"Still chasing that hoop dream, Elijah?" Darius asked, his eyes cold despite his smile. "Why break your back for the pros when you could be living large right now?"

Elijah stood his ground, aware of Marcus's nervousness beside him. "That's not my song, Darius. You know that."

The situation could have gotten ugly if not for the arrival of a man in an AAU tracksuit. "Everything cool here?" he asked, his eyes scanning Elijah and Darius.

Darius and his crew faded back into the night, and the man introduced himself as Coach Johnson. "I've been watching you play, Elijah. You've got talent. I want to put your skills on display at a bigger stage."

As Coach Johnson explained the opportunity before him, a chance to be seen by college scouts at an upcoming AAU tournament, Elijah felt a new beat drop in his chest. This was it, the bridge to a new verse in his life's song.

That night when Elijah told his mom, he saw a mix of pride and fear in her eyes. She wrapped him in a tight hug; her voice choked with emotion. "You play your

FOR THE LOVE OF THE GAME

heart out, baby. Show them what Camden is made of."

As Elijah lay in bed that night the two melodies of hope and fear played in his head. The road ahead was unclear, full of promise and danger. But as he fell asleep Elijah knew he was ready to face the music to play his part in a much bigger song.

C. GROOMS & BOBBY MAY

Chapter 3: Canton's Calling

The pre-dawn cold clung to Clifford Michaels as he walked the empty streets of Canton, Ohio. The ball in his hands was a steady heartbeat in a world of offbeat.

As Clifford got to the court he started his routine, each movement a note in his melody. The ball bouncing on the asphalt muffled the doubts in his head that said kids from Canton don't make it.

The sun was just starting to rise when a voice pierced Clifford's focus. "Damn, Cliff. You trying to wear a hole in the court?"

Clifford turned to see his boy Darnell standing on the sidelines. He caught the ball and walked over, noticing the look of indecision in Darnell's eyes.

"Just getting in work, D. You know how it is."

Darnell nodded but there was a weight to his voice that Clifford couldn't ignore. "I know, man. But… there's more than one way to get out of Canton."

FOR THE LOVE OF THE GAME

The silence between them was heavy. Clifford had seen it before, friends and neighbors turning to the streets, chasing the quick buck, and trying to escape from poverty.

"I'm not interested, Darnell," Clifford said flatly. "That's not my thing"

Darnell sighed, disappointed and worry on his face. "I hear you. Just keep your options open, okay? The basketball dream is a long shot."

As Darnell walked away his words stuck in Clifford's head. A long shot. Wasn't that his whole life? Born to a single mother in a town where dreams went to die, every step towards his goal felt like trying to move a mountain.

Clifford was about to get back to work when his phone buzzed. The text he read made his heart skip a beat: an invitation to the AAU showcase in Atlanta, a chance to play in front of college coaches and scouts.

C. GROOMS & BOBBY MAY

As the reality of it all hit him, Clifford felt a mix of excitement and fear. This was the moment he'd been waiting for, the chance to prove his long shot would hit.

He ran home, burst through the door with more energy than he had after hours of practice. "Mom! Mom, you won't believe it!"

His mom came out of the kitchen, the worry lines on her face smoothing out as she saw her son's face. As Clifford told her the news, he watched hope grow in her eyes, all the hard work and sacrifices of the years coming to this moment.

"Oh, Cliff," she whispered, hugging him tight. "I'm so proud of you. You're going to do remarkable things."

That night as Clifford lay in bed his mind was racing. The showcase in Atlanta was the biggest stage of his career and the opportunity was filled with uncertainty.

FOR THE LOVE OF THE GAME

Chapter 4: Harmony in Atlanta

The AAU showcase was buzzing, a symphony of squeaking sneakers, bouncing balls, coaches, and players yelling. Malik, Elijah, and Clifford were on the same court together, each aware of the others' greatness.

As the game got more intense their individual sounds started to mesh, creating a sound none of them had ever heard before. Malik's smooth ball handling was the beat, Elijah's explosive drives were the punch, Clifford's sharp shooting was the melody.

In the heat of competition a connection was made. They moved like they'd been playing together for years, their styles meshing in ways they never could have imagined.

After the game they caught their breath on the sidelines and Malik spoke up. "Man that was something else. I'm Malik, from Harlem."

"Elijah, Camden, New Jersey."

"Clifford, Canton, Ohio."

They spent the rest of the showcase pushing each other to get better. As the event ended, they exchanged numbers and a silent agreement that they had made something special.

Weeks later as they were each considering their college options, a group text went off.

Malik: "What do y'all think about Georgetown University ?"

Elijah: "Got an offer from them yesterday. You too?"

Clifford: "Same here. Their program looks solid."

Malik: "What if we did this? For real? Could be something special."

There was a pause as the weight of the suggestion settled.

Elijah: "I'm in if you are."

Clifford: "Let's do it."

FOR THE LOVE OF THE GAME

As they made their decisions each felt the magnitude of the moment. They were not just choosing a college; they were choosing to do this together. Malik thought of Harlem, Masterson and PHP, and the weight of his community's expectations. Elijah thought of Camden's streets, of the path he was leaving behind. Clifford thought of Canton, of his mother's sacrifices, of the future he was fighting to create.

Their phones buzzed one last time that night:

Malik: "This is it. No turning back now."

Elijah: "Together, all the way."

Clifford: "Georgetown University won't know what hit them."

As they put their phones down in their respective hometowns a sense of anticipation filled the air. The future stretched out before them full of promise and possibility. Georgetown University was waiting and with it the chance to play on a bigger stage than they'd ever known.

C. GROOMS & BOBBY MAY

In Harlem Malik could hear PHP beats pulsing through the thin walls, Masterson still working. In Camden Elijah took one last look at the street corner where he'd stood down Darius. And in Canton Clifford ran his hand over the worn leather of his basketball, a sign of the journey to come.

Tomorrow will bring more struggles, more victories, more trials. But for now on the eve of the biggest change of their lives, they allowed themselves to take in a breath of pure unadulterated hope. The game that had brought them together would take them further than they had ever imagined.

Chapter 5: Courtside Connections

The bass was thumping through the studio walls, the beat pulsing like a heartbeat. Masterson and his crew, PHP, were huddled around the mixing board, their faces lit up by the computer screen.

"That's it," Masterson said, grinning. "That's the beat we've been looking for."

The group nodded, smiling. They were going hard on different tracks for weeks.

Malik was sitting in the corner, his heart full of pride. He'd always known his brother had talent, but seeing him in his zone, creating something sick was a beautiful thing. But concern lingered. The music industry was ruthless and full of temptations that could sidetrack even the most talented artists.

"Malik, what you think?" Masterson asked, snapping him out of his trance. "Is this the one?"

Malik forced a smile. "It's fire, Mass. You guys killed it."

Masterson grinned. "Wait till you see us perform it live. We're opening for one of the biggest names in the game."

Malik's eyes went wide. "That's huge. Congrats, Mass."

As PHP's star continued to rise, Malik's unease grew. He had his own dreams to chase, but he wanted to support his brother every step of the way.

After a long USA Basketball training camp, Malik, Elijah, and Clifford were sitting in Malik's living room, talking about upcoming games, and listening to Masterson's new track. Malik was caught between two worlds.

"I'm happy for you, Mass," Elijah said, genuinely smiling. "You've been working and it's paying off."

Clifford nodded. "We'll support you, just like you support us."

Malik smiled but was struggling to keep it together. He knew firsthand the temptations and distractions of success and was worried about the same for his brother.

"Mass, I'm worried about you," Malik said one night. "This industry can be cruel."

Masterson sighed. "I know you're looking out for me, but I can take care of myself."

"It's not about you being a kid. It's about the people around you," Malik said, his voice full of feeling.

Masterson nodded. "I appreciate your concern but trust me. If I need help, I'll come to you first."

Malik's heart was full of pride and fear. He had to let his brother figure it out on his own.

As the weeks went by, Malik threw himself into training. He had his own goals and wanted to motivate his brother. PHP's big show arrived, the venue was packed, and the energy was high. Masterson and his crew were nervous backstage but ready.

"Yo, this is it," Masterson said. "Our time to show the world what we're made of."

Malik, Elijah, and Clifford watched from the wings, pride and anxiety mixed. The crowd went wild as PHP hit the stage, the energy in the room was electric. Malik's heart was full of pride but also worry.

After the show, Masterson was surrounded by fans and industry people. Malik watched, proud but protective.

"Malik, did you see that?" Masterson asked. "We killed it!"

"You were great, Mass. I'm so proud of you," Malik said.

Masterson grinned. "I couldn't have done it without you. You've always had my back."

"I'll always be there for you, no matter what," Malik said.

FOR THE LOVE OF THE GAME

"I know, Malik. I won't let you down. I know how to handle this industry."

As the months went by, PHP's star kept rising. But with success came the temptations. Malik worried about his brother's well-being, seeing shady characters offering shortcuts to success.

One night, after a hard practice, Malik told Elijah and Clifford, "I want to be there for him, but I feel like I'm losing him to this world."

Elijah nodded. "You can't control everything. Masterson has to figure it out on his own."

Clifford added, "Maybe he needs this journey to come out stronger."

"We'll be there for him, Malik," Elijah said. "Just like we've always been there for each other."

Malik felt a sense of relief washing over him. He made a silent promise: no matter what, he would always be there for Masterson. United by unbreakable ties, they would face the future together, in the worlds of sports and music, each making their own way but supporting each other every step of the way.

Chapter 6: Rising Stars

The locker room was silent as a tomb, electric with anticipation. Malik, Elijah, and Clifford sat side by side, heads down, ready for the game of their lives.

Malik's mind wandered to Harlem where he spent hours on neighborhood courts under the summer sun. He remembered his mom's unwavering support despite her two jobs to put food on the table. "You were born for this, Malik," she'd say, her eyes shining.

Elijah thought back to Camden where he escaped the violence through basketball. He remembered his dad's initial doubt: "You think you're going to make it out of here playing ball?" But Elijah's determination eventually won his dad over.

Clifford thought of his childhood in Canton and his single mom's sacrifices. He remembered making the prestigious AAU team and his mom crying tears of joy.

As they sat there, lost in thought, they felt a bond and shared purpose. Elijah spoke up, "Remember when we first met at that AAU tournament? We were all so nervous." Malik smiled, "Yeah, then we killed it. I knew we had something." Clifford added, "And then we made the USA team and everything changed."

They talked about the long hours of practice, the tough competition, and the brotherhood with their teammates. "That was a turning point," Malik said. "It showed us what we were capable of." Elijah nodded, "And now we're about to play the game of our lives." Clifford stood up, his eyes were fierce. "Let's show them what we're made of. Let's make our families proud." Malik and Elijah nodded, their eyes matching his.

As they stepped onto the court, Malik's mind went back to his early high school days balancing basketball and academics with college recruitment. He thought about his mom's sacrifices for his dreams. Elijah thought about his high school struggles, studying hard for college scholarships with

FOR THE LOVE OF THE GAME

his dad's extra work. Clifford thought about his AAU days, the competition and the game winner that defined his fate. The game was underway, and Malik, Elijah and Clifford were in sync. The score was close, and the pressure was on. In the final minutes Malik drove to the basket and scored giving them a two-point lead. The crowd went wild, Elijah yelled, "That was all you, Malik!" Clifford patted him on the back, "You're going to be a legend." As the final buzzer sounded and they won, Malik was in awe and gratitude. They had proved themselves and risen above their circumstances. In the locker room Malik's eyes welled up with tears and he thanked his teammates for their unwavering support. "We're in this together," Elijah said. "We'll always remember where we came from."

Malik felt at peace and grateful. He knew more was ahead but with his teammates and family he was ready. As they walked out of the arena the crowd still echoing in their ears Malik felt unstoppable. This was his time, and he was going to go after his dreams one game at a time.

C. GROOMS & BOBBY MAY

Chapter 7: College Bound

The sun was setting over the city as Malik, Elijah and Clifford connected on a video call on the rooftop. They needed a minute of peace from the chaos of college recruitment and high school graduation prep.

"Can you believe it?" Malik said, breaking the silence. "We're high school graduates in a few hours."

Elijah nodded, smiling. "We've come a long way. Just a few years ago we were kids playing ball in the park."

Clifford laughed. "And now every top program wants us. It's like a dream."

They sat in silence for a moment, thinking about their journey. Despite going to different high schools, they were always available for each other and supported each other through the tough times.

"Remember our first AAU tournament?" Malik asked. "We were so nervous about messing up in front of the scouts."

Elijah smiled. "Yeah, and then you scored 30 points like it was nothing. That's when I knew we had something special."

Clifford smiled. "We've come a long way. Look at our stats from this season. We were unstoppable even at different schools."

Their accomplishments hung in the air. They had given up so much to chase their basketball dreams. Now, on the cusp of college, uncertainty was looming.

"Have you thought about the NBA?" Malik asked nervously. "It's always been my dream. With how we've been playing it feels possible."

Elijah and Clifford stared deep in thought and seemed like they were suspended in time for a few seconds. They shared Malik's dream but knew the path to the NBA wasn't guaranteed.

"It's tempting," Elijah said. "But a college education is important too, a backup plan in case things don't work out."

Clifford nodded. "There's no guarantee any of us will get drafted and we need something to fall back on. However, and I mean this wholeheartedly, if any of would get drafted it would be you, Malik."

Malik rubbed his hand over his head and was humbled that his peers believed in him. School was definitely important to him, but he would surely go pro if the opportunity presented itself.

"I hear you," he said, firm. "I know college is important, but I don't want to let this slip away. I have to consider it."

Elijah and Clifford knew how much this meant to Malik.

"We got your back, Malik, no matter what happens" Elijah said, smiling.

Clifford nodded, his eyes intense. "Who knows, maybe we'll all end up in the league together someday. I'm willing to chase the dream."

FOR THE LOVE OF THE GAME

Malik felt a lump in his throat; he was also emotional and grateful to his friends who believed in him.

The next few weeks were a whirlwind of college recruitment. Malik, Elijah, and Clifford researched schools, talked to coaches, and weighed their options. Eventually they stuck with their original pick: Georgetown University with its top tier academics, rich basketball history, and it was always at the top of their list. It seemed like a perfect fit. They had talked about it briefly in the past and considered attending together but now the moment was right in front of them.

They linked up on another video call before meeting up, "It's time to do this," Malik said in a fully committed tone "This is everything we asked for."

Elijah's eyes widened because of the gravity of the moment "This is a surreal feeling like we're in a movie. Athletic scholarships aside, it's extremely hard to get in this school and we qualified academically first."

Clifford smiled. "We've worked for this. Now it's time to show what we're made of."

Recapping their visit, a few things came to mind; In spite of the racial disparity in its demographic makeup, Georgetown University felt like home. It wasn't a typical official visit where you are shuttled around the various facilities and everyone knew your name. There was a uniqueness about the campus and its place in the city didn't go unnoticed. Nestled in the urban pocket that is D.C., but the seclusion and illusion of hiding in plain sight couldn't be overlooked either. The people were nice, the facilities were great, and the community was strong. They signed their letters of intent and made it official. There was a lot to live up to as well so the pressure to succeed would never be minimized or taken for granted.

"We want you to be part of something special here," coach Thompson said. "We believe in your talent and your potential and will help you reach your goals."

FOR THE LOVE OF THE GAME

Malik felt a lump in his throat again. "Thank you, Coach. This means more than you know."

Elijah and Clifford nodded, and their eyes were shining with gratitude. This was their chance to go after their dreams and make a difference.

They were about to enter a new world and make their mark. Malik, Elijah, and Clifford felt a sense of excitement for what was to come. They were college bound and ready for whatever was next, but dreams don't keep the lights on.

C. GROOMS & BOBBY MAY

Chapter 8: Shattered Dreams

Three months later, the locker room was electric but there was also some tension as Malik, Elijah and Clifford walked in. Coach Thompson stood at the front with the assistant coaches and some stern-looking school officials.

"Sit down," Coach Thompson said. "We have some urgent and pressing business to discuss."

Malik looked at his teammates and his mind was racing but he couldn't understand why.

"What's going on Coach?" Elijah asked.

Coach Thompson let out a deep breath and scanned the room before focusing on them. "Our program is under investigation and there are allegations of illegal recruitment and payments to players."

Gasps and murmurs quickly filled the room. Malik's stomach dropped. "What do you mean illegal recruitment?" Clifford asked, his voice rising. "We didn't do anything wrong!"

FOR THE LOVE OF THE GAME

Coach Thompson held up his hand, his face serious. "Two players that graduated last year were allegedly part of a pay-for-play scandal. They were alleged to have received cars, houses, jobs, and cash in exchange for signing with certain schools because of sneaker affiliations."

Malik's mind was racing with confusion and betrayal. He had trusted Coach Thompson completely and this was too much to handle. How could he not know about this and that it would be an issue before they decided to sign with the school?

"How could this happen?" Elijah whispered, his voice shaking. "How could they do this to us?"

Coach Thompson's shoulders slumped. "I know this is tough, but we're going to get to the bottom of this and make it right. We'll cooperate fully with the investigation."

Malik's throat was tight with anger. "What about us, Coach? What happens to us now?"

C. GROOMS & BOBBY MAY

Coach Thompson looked regretful. "Our program will likely get sanctioned, and your scholarships may be affected. But we'll fight for you and be with you through this entire process."

In the days that followed, the scandal made national news, and Georgetown University was in the headlines for all the wrong reasons. Malik, Elijah, and Clifford were in the middle of a media ambush and every move they made was being watched.

As the investigation continued, they met with lawyers and investigators. The pressure was mounting, and fear of their involvement was growing.

"What if they try to pin this on us?" Elijah asked, his voice shaking. "What if they say we knew and didn't say anything?"

Malik's jaw clenched. "We have to stay strong and stick together. We know the truth and we just have to trust it will come out." Despite their determination the scandal was taking a toll on their mental and emotional health. Malik was withdrawing from his

FOR THE LOVE OF THE GAME

family, too ashamed to face their questions. Elijah was struggling with depression and self-doubt. Clifford was furious with the system and the coaches who had betrayed their trust. As weeks turned into months the three faced a crossroads. The program was suspended, and a few scholarships were taken away. "Maybe we should transfer," Elijah said, his voice defeat. "Start over somewhere else."

Clifford shook his head. "No way. We can't let the system win. We have to stay and fight, clear our names, and restore the program's integrity." Malik was quiet, thinking. Transferring would be easy, an escape from the spotlight. But running wouldn't solve their problems.

"Clifford's right," he said finally, his voice firm. "We have to stay and prove that we're not cheaters and liars."

Elijah and Clifford nodded, agreeing with Malik. They knew the road would be long and hard, but they trusted they could get through it together.

C. GROOMS & BOBBY MAY

Chapter 9: Brotherhood Tested

The team struggled to stay focused, but Malik, Elijah and Clifford were constantly displaying leadership and helping to keep their season afloat. They were high-fiving and hugging after a hard-won victory. Adrenaline was pumping through their veins.

Underneath it all, Malik was seething. He'd been on the bench most of the game and felt his talent was being wasted. As the team was leaving the locker room, Elijah pulled Malik aside. "Hey man, you, okay? You seemed off today. Talk to me."

Malik shrugged, grinding his teeth. "I'm fine. Just frustrated. I feel like I'm not getting the opportunities I deserve."

Elijah looked at him surprised. "What do you mean? You're one of the most important parts of this team. How you go we go. At this stage of the season, do I really have to tell you that? C'mon man. If you struggle, we still have your back. The team is stepping up and holding down the fort for you "

FOR THE LOVE OF THE GAME

"Am I though? From where I sit it feels like I'm just a benchwarmer in crunch time when it matters the most."

Elijah's face got hard. "Don't say some bullshit like that man. We're all in this together."

"Easy for you to say. You're starting every game, getting all the glory. I'm stuck on the bench, watching my dreams disappear."

Elijah stepped back, hurt. "You're being so selfish, Malik. This isn't just about you. It's about the team."

Clifford jumped in, holding up his hands. "Whoa, whoa. Let's calm down. We're all on the same team. Both of you calm the hell down! What's going on?"

The tension between the three friends grew over the next few days. Elijah was struggling to balance his school work with basketball and was falling behind in his classes and withdrew from the team. Even as the consummate team player and level-headed one, Clifford was dealing with his own issues. His father's constant criticism was affecting his mental health and lately he was snapping at his teammates.

After practice one day Elijah confronted Clifford. "What's going on with you? You've been on edge all week. What's really good with you?"

Clifford bristled. "I don't know what you're talking about. I'm just focusing on my game and trying to be a leader for this team. I'm out here busting my ass just like you."

"It's more than that man. You're pushing yourself a little too hard. You need a break. Basketball isn't everything."

Clifford's face got red with anger. "That's easy for you to say. You're not the one with a father breathing down your neck every second. You don't know what it's like to have that kind of pressure."

"You're right, I don't. But you can't keep going like this. It's not healthy."

FOR THE LOVE OF THE GAME

Clifford's shoulders slumped. "I know. I feel like I'm drowning, and I don't know how to come up for air. Damn!"

Elijah put his hand on his friend's shoulder. "You don't have to do this alone. We're here for you. Me and Malik, we've got your back."

Clifford nodded, his eyes welling up. "Thanks, man. I really appreciate that. I'm a good student in one of the best programs in the nation and trying to make a mark in life. I'm constantly trying to get better but pops always on my ass."

Meanwhile Malik decided to talk to the coach about his role. "Coach, I feel like my talents are being wasted on the bench when the team needs me. Are you giving up on me?"

Coach Thompson looked at him with a serious look.

"I understand your frustration, but you have to trust the process. You're the best player on the team but even the best can struggle. I need you to see past yourself and look at the big picture.

C. GROOMS & BOBBY MAY

"That's not good enough coach. I need to be out there all the time contributing to the team. I can't work through my struggles on the bench in crunch time. You say I'm the best, then treat me as such."

"Listen son, if you can't be a team player then you can't be on this team, and I need you to never lose sight of that."

Malik's eyes widened, and at that moment he realized the consequences of his actions. He left the coach's office and ran into Elijah and Clifford.

"I messed up. I let my ego get in the way and now I don't know what's going to happen going forward."

Clifford put his hand on his shoulder. "We've all been there. We all have our moments of weakness. But we'll get through this together. You have to trust the process."

Elijah nodded. "We've been through too much to let this tear us apart. We need to have each other's backs."

FOR THE LOVE OF THE GAME

The three friends started having real conversations, opening up about their struggles and fears. Elijah talked about his school work. Clifford talked about his father. Malik apologized for being selfish.

They re-committed to having each other's backs, on and off the court. Their next game, they played with more passion and energy. As the final buzzer sounded and they won, Malik, Elijah and Clifford hugged each other, tears of joy streaming down their faces.

They had passed a major test on the road to adulthood Malik felt confident that they would be all right, no matter what came next, as long as they had each other. Counseling, mediation, and mentorship go a long way in sports and in life.

C. GROOMS & BOBBY MAY

Chapter 10: Courtside Ambitions

The next game, Malik, Elijah, and Clifford prepared themselves for the biggest games of their college careers up to that point, the conference championship. The atmosphere crackled with a mix of nerves and excitement. The gym was buzzing with an unmatched energy and volume as the gym rumbled beneath the feet.

As they completed their game routines, they reminisced about their journey, meeting on the AAU circuit bonding over their shared passion for the game and enduring tough practices and intense competitions in high school basketball. They also recalled the scandal that was also derailing their college careers and the unyielding loyalty that bound them together.

"Remember when we first played together?" Elijah asked with a grin. "We were kids with big dreams."

FOR THE LOVE OF THE GAME

Clifford chuckled. "Yeah. One game away from becoming champions."

Malik nodded, his eyes filled with determination. "We've made strides. Our mission isn't over yet. We need to see this through to the end."

Coach Thompsons voice broke through the noise, in the locker room. "Gather 'round, boys. I have something to share."

The team huddled together in a circle, their expressions solemn as they listened intently.

"I know this season has been a ride " Coach Thompson started his voice tinged with emotion.

"You've exemplified redemption and loyalty. We've formed a bond, like family. Let's now display the essence of Georgetown University basketball to the world. Take a moment to get your thoughts together and let's lock in and focus. We're here now. The moment of truth."

C. GROOMS & BOBBY MAY

Malik felt a lump in his throat. "We owe it all to you Coach. Let's do it!" Elijah's words shook the locker room.

A smile graced Coach Thompsons face and his eyes simmered with emotion.

"That's what family is about. Let's go out there and make our mark. TEAM ON 3. HOYAS ON 6!"

As they stepped onto the court the arena hummed with excitement. Malik sensed the gravity of the moment and pushed aside any jitters. He had put in too much effort to let his anxiety take over.

The game kicked off energetically with both teams exchanging baskets. Malik moved with finesse and maneuvered past defenders effortlessly. However, as the game progressed, challenges emerged. Elijah showed signs of discomfort, while Clifford faced the tough assignment of guarding the opponent's best player and leading scorer during the tournament.

FOR THE LOVE OF THE GAME

During a break, in play Malik gathered them together. "We need to stay focused guys. Don't let them mess with our heads. Cliff, we need you to dig in. We got your back."

Elijah nodded determinedly through the pain he was enduring. "I'll push through it no matter what."

Clifford took a breath and asserted confidently " I won't allow him to affect me mentally. I got you."

As they made their way back to the court Malik still felt some uncertainty. The gravity of the moment was definitely weighing on him heavily. He was their best player, and he had a flashback to his confrontation with a coach Thompson. Elijah and Clifford stood by his side and snapped him out of his trance. Their eyes were filled with determination and Clifford's words pierced through the deafening sounds of the arena, "Malik, bring us home brother!"

"Don't worry" Malik reassured Elijah. "I'm all in."

C. GROOMS & BOBBY MAY

Clifford nodded in agreement and shouted, "NO DOUBT"

They dove back into the game trading the lead back and forth as tension mounted in the arena with each possession.

In one of the moments Elijah lunged for a ball out of bounds with a heroic effort to secure the possession. Clifford caught the pass and was fouled underneath the basket. He calmly sank two free throws to put them back in front. A half court heave from the other team hit the back of the rim and bounced off as the crowd erupted as the buzzer sounded. Malik, Elijah, and Clifford embraced each other tightly as tears of happiness streamed down their faces.

In the locker room amid the jubilation, Malik, Elijah, and Clifford found a corner where emotions ran high. "We pulled it off " said Clifford with tears still in his eyes.

FOR THE LOVE OF THE GAME

Elijah smiled broadly. "This is what we've been trying to do for the entire season and having you all by my side to do it means the world to me "

Malik expressed gratefully. "I wouldn't have been able to accomplish this without your support. You've been my pillars of strength throughout everything. I love both of you more than words can express"

Clifford chimed in quickly, "Do you love me enough to get me a steak and cheese gyro later?" They just laughed.

In that embrace they understood that this moment would remain etched in their memories forever. A true testament to the bond that they shared.

Reflecting on their journey, they realized the significance of loyalty, determination, and companionship. Looking ahead they were aware that new obstacles awaited them. However armed with their connection they believed they could conquer anything.

C. GROOMS & BOBBY MAY

"What's our next move?" Clifford inquired eagerly.

Elijah replied with a shrug and a grin "The world is ours for the taking."

Malik concurred, "Regardless of where life takes us, we will always have each other's back."

Standing united reveling in their triumph, they acknowledged that their adventure was far from complete. They were more than teammates—they were a family. Together there was no limit to what they could achieve.

FOR THE LOVE OF THE GAME

Chapter 11: The Business of Basketball 101

Coach Thompson leaned back in his leather office chair and his eyes came into focus as he stared out the window at the Georgetown University campus. The setting sun cast long shadows across the quad, mirroring the dark thoughts creeping into his mind. He found himself transported back to a conversation a decade ago, one that had opened his eyes to the rapidly evolving and increasingly corrupt landscape of youth basketball.

The memory was vivid: a small coffee shop in D.C., the aroma of freshly brewed coffee mingling with the low hum of conversation. Across from him sat Jimmy Smalls, his childhood friend and now a rising star in the world of youth basketball. Jimmy's eyes had sparkled with ambition as he leaned across the table, his voice low but intense.

"I'm creating an AAU Tournament program that will revolutionize the game," Jimmy said, his extreme excitement was almost uncontrollable. "The Above the Rim Basketball Promotional Program. We're going to change everything, John."

Coach Thompson listened, both intrigued and unsettled, as Jimmy laid out his vision. "We'll recruit players based on their allegiance to sneaker companies," Jimmy explained. "Five all-star teams in each major market, New York, Pennsylvania, Texas, Ohio, and California. Each team will have 12 players, all affiliated with the specific brands of Adidas, Nike, Reebok, New Balance, or Puma."

"That's quite an undertaking," Coach Thompson had replied, his coaching instincts already raising red flags. "Walk me through the financials, Jimmy. How do you plan to make this sustainable?"

Jimmy's response was a masterclass in the economics of youth sports. He pulled out a meticulously organized folder and laid his spreadsheets across the table. "We'll have 10 invited teams per state, each paying $10,000. That's $500,000 in entry fees alone."

FOR THE LOVE OF THE GAME

Coach Thompson's eyebrows had risen at the figure, but Jimmy was just getting started. "The sponsors will pay for prime advertisement placements in each state's tournament. I was thinking $30,000 per sponsor, with 30 sponsors per state, that's an additional $4,500,000."

The numbers had made Coach Thompson's head spin, but Jimmy wasn't done. "We'll have 50 AAU coaches, each receiving a stipend of $1,000 per week. Over 50 weeks, that's $2.5 million in stipends. That would leave me well over 2 million dollars in discretionary funds."

"That's a hefty sum, Jimmy," Coach Thompson said, his unease growing. "How do you plan to use the discretionary funds?"

Jimmy smiled, a glint in his eye that Coach Thompson now recognized as a warning sign. "I'll use the funds as I see fit but some of it will go to paying the tournament staff to manage the games and the officiating unions who will provide the refs. To bring in more income, we'll have 500 college coaches paying $5,000 in advance for entry into the event, and another 100 coaches paying $10,000 for VIP All Access. So, that's $2.25 million in coaches' fees plus the $2.5 million in discretionary funds which is $4.75 million in net income."

Coach Thompson had done the mental math, his coaching instincts warring with his business sense. "So you're looking at revenue of almost $8 million, with expenses around $3 million. That's a net profit of nearly $5 million per event."

"Exactly, Coach," Jimmy had replied, his grin widening. "And as the program gains traction, those numbers will only grow."

As the memory faded, Coach Thompson felt a chill running down his spine. He'd been naive then, impressed by Jimmy's business acumen but blind to the implications. Now, with the benefit of hindsight and the weight of an impending scandal pressing down on college basketball, he saw that conversation in a vastly different light.

The reality of Jimmy's operation, as Coach Thompson had come to understand over the years, was far more complex and insidious than that initial conversation had suggested. What Jimmy had presented as a revolutionary approach to youth basketball had evolved into a labyrinth of financial manipulation and ethical compromises.

At the heart of Jimmy's empire was a network of Limited Liability Companies (LLCs) and shell corporations, each designed to obscure the flow of money. On the surface, it all looked legitimate grassroots basketball at its finest, providing opportunities for young talent to shine. But beneath that veneer lay a web of financial manipulation that would make a Wall Street banker blush.

Payments to families were disguised as consulting fees, routed through multiple companies before reaching their final destination. A parent might receive a check from "Midwest Youth Sports Development LLC" for "community outreach services," the connection to their child's basketball career hidden beneath layers of corporate bureaucracy.

Coach Thompson had pieced together the structure over years of careful observation and discreet inquiries. The Above the Rim Basketball Promotional Program was just the beginning. Below the surface lay a complex network of seemingly unrelated businesses:

1. Slam Dunk Marketing Solutions LLC
2. Hoops Dreams Consulting Group
3. Baseline Ventures Inc.
4. Fast Break Financial Services
5. Full Court Press Media Group

Each of these entities played a crucial role in the movement and laundering of funds. Sponsorship money from sneaker companies, for instance, wouldn't go directly to the Above the Rim program. Instead, it might start at Slam Dunk Marketing

Solutions, move through Hoops Dreams Consulting for "event planning services," then to Baseline Ventures for "talent development," before finally reaching its intended recipients.

The amounts involved were staggering. Coach Thompson had initially been impressed by Jimmy's projection of $5 million in net revenue. But as the program grew, so did the cash flow. Within five years, the Annual Above the Rim Championship was generating over $20 million in net revenue, with only a fraction of that reported publicly.

The tournament itself was a masterpiece of misdirection. While the entry fees ($500,000) and general admission tickets and concession sales (another $500,000) were publicly reported, they were merely the tip of the iceberg. The real money flowed through back channels:

- "VIP Experiences" for college coaches: Ostensibly priced at $5,000-$10,000, these packages often included under-the-table payments of up to $50,000 for access to top recruits.

- "Equipment Sponsorships": What appeared to be $10,000 deals to provide gear for teams often included additional $25,000-$100,000 payments directly to players or their families.

- "Consulting Fees": Parents of top players could earn anywhere from $5,000 to $250,000 per year for vague services like "community outreach" or "talent scouting."

All of these transactions were carefully structured to appear innocent in isolation. A payment from Fast Break Financial Services to a player's parent for "financial advisory services" wouldn't raise eyebrows. Neither would a consulting fee from Full Court Press Media Group for "media training." But together, they formed a pattern of systematic exploitation of young athletes and their immediate families.

The scale of the operation was mind-boggling. Coach Thompson's sources suggested that in the last fiscal

FOR THE LOVE OF THE GAME

year alone, over $30 million had flowed through Jimmy's network of companies. Of that, less than a third was publicly accounted for. The rest vanished into a black hole of offshore accounts, real estate investments, and cash payments.

As he contemplated the enormity of the deception, Coach Thompson's stomach churned. How many young lives had been impacted by this system? How many dreams had been corrupted by the allure of easy money?

He thought of his own players, Malik, Elijah, Clifford, and the passion and integrity they brought to the game. They were the reason he coached, the reason he still believed in the transformative power of basketball despite the corruption that threatened to engulf it.

But for every Malik, Elijah, and Clifford, there were dozens of young athletes caught in Jimmy's web. Coach Thompson had seen the consequences firsthand:

- Talented players choosing schools based on under-the-table payments rather than academic or athletic fit.
- Families becoming dependent on the influx of cash, pressuring their children to prioritize basketball over education.
- Young athletes develop a skewed sense of value, equating their worth with the size of the checks they could command.

The long-term implications were even more troubling. Players who didn't make it to the NBA often found themselves adrift, their education neglected in pursuit of a pro career that never materialized. Even those who did make it to the league were often ill-equipped to handle their sudden wealth, having been conditioned to see money as easy come, easy go.

And yet, the system has persisted. The allure of profit was too strong, the potential for exploitation too tempting. Coaches, shoe companies, agents, and yes, even some parents, all had their hands out, eager for a piece of the pie.

FOR THE LOVE OF THE GAME

As the last rays of sunlight faded from his office, Coach Thompson felt the weight of his knowledge pressing down on him. He had always prided himself on running a clean program, on developing not just athletes, but well-rounded young men. But in the face of such systemic corruption, was that enough?

He thought back again to his conversation with Jimmy all those years ago. Had his friend always intended for things to go this far? Or had he, like so many others, been seduced by the promise of easy money and lost sight of what truly mattered?

With a heavy sigh, Coach Thompson turned to the tasks at hand. He had a team to prepare, strategies to devise, and a legacy to build. The business of basketball would continue to evolve, often in ways that tested the very spirit of the game. But as long as there were coaches and players who remembered why they fell in love with basketball in the first place, there was hope.

C. GROOMS & BOBBY MAY

As he gathered his papers and prepared to leave, Coach Thompson made a silent vow. He would do everything in his power to protect his players from the darker aspects of the game, to help them see beyond the allure of quick money and fleeting fame. Because in the end, it wasn't about the basketball business more than it was about the love of the game itself.

The memory of his conversation with Jimmy Smalls lingered, a stark reminder of how far the world of youth basketball had strayed from its roots. But it also served as a call to action to those who still believed in the purity of the game.

As he switched off his office light and stepped into the hallway, Coach Thompson felt a renewed sense of purpose. The fight for the soul of basketball was far from over, and he was ready to lead the charge. He couldn't change the entire system overnight, but he could make a difference in the lives of the young men under his care. He could teach them not just how to play the game, but how to navigate the complex and often treacherous world that surrounded it.

FOR THE LOVE OF THE GAME

Tomorrow, he will step onto the court with a new perspective. He would look at each of his players not just as athletes, but as young men standing at a crossroads. And he would do everything in his power to guide them down the right path, to show them that true success wasn't measured in dollars and cents, but in the impact, they could have on the world around them.

The business of basketball had become a tangled web of money and influence. However, the game itself, with the squeak of sneakers on the hardwood, the swish of a perfect shot, and the camaraderie of a team working as one, remained pure. And as long as that purity existed, there was something worth fighting for.

Coach Thompson locked his office door, his resolve strengthened. The path ahead would be difficult and filled with ethical dilemmas. But he was ready to face it head-on, armed with the wisdom of experience and the unwavering belief in the power of the game he loved.

C. GROOMS & BOBBY MAY

As he walked out into the cool night air, the campus quiet around him, Coach Thompson felt a glimmer of hope. The business of basketball had changed, but the heart of the game remained the same. And as long as there were those willing to stand up for what was right, to prioritize integrity over profit and character over cash, basketball would continue to transform lives for the better.

With that thought elevating his spirits, Coach Thompson headed home, ready to face whatever tomorrow might bring. Basketball might be complex and often corrupt, but the game itself, and the positive impact it could have on young people's lives, was simple and pure. And that was something worth dedicating his life to.

FOR THE LOVE OF THE GAME

Chapter 12: Off-Court Challenges

The early morning sun filtered through the curtains of Malik's dorm room, casting a warm glow on his face as he stirred awake. His phone buzzed insistently, pulling him from his slumber. Squinting at the bright screen, he saw a text from an unknown number:

"Hey Malik, it's Jasmine. We met at the party last weekend. Want to grab coffee sometime?"

Malik sat up, suddenly wide awake. Memories of Jasmine flooded his mind with her infectious laugh, her sparkling eyes, and the hours they'd spent in deep conversation. An instant connection had sparked between them, but now, in the harsh light of day, guilt gnawed at him.

Basketball was his focus, his ticket to the NBA. Distractions weren't part of the plan.

With a heavy sigh, Malik typed out a response: "Hey Jasmine, it was great meeting you too. I'm really busy with basketball right now. Maybe we can get together some other time?"

He tossed his phone aside, the weight of his decision settling uncomfortably in his chest. As he changed into his practice gear, Malik pushed thoughts of Jasmine to the back of his mind. The court was calling, and he couldn't afford to let anything, or anyone, derail his dreams.

Across campus, Elijah faced a different kind of struggle. His phone rang, his mother's worried voice on the other end delivering news that felt like a punch to the gut: his younger sister, Maya, had been arrested for shoplifting.

"Maya? How could this happen?" Elijah asked, his voice barely above a whisper.

His mother's sigh crackled through the phone. "I don't know, Elijah. She's always been such a good kid. I just... I don't understand."

FOR THE LOVE OF THE GAME

Before Elijah could respond, his phone beeped with another incoming call. It was Maya.

"I'll call you back, Mom," he said quickly, switching to the other line. "Maya, what's going on?"

His sister's voice was small, choked with tears. "I'm so sorry, Elijah. I didn't mean to do it. I just... I didn't know what else to do."

Confusion and concern warred within Elijah. "What do you mean? Maya, talk to me."

"It's Dad," Maya whispered, the words seeming to physically pain her. "He lost his job. We're struggling so much. I just wanted to help Mom. I messed up."

Elijah's heart sank. He knew things had been tight at home, but he hadn't realized the extent of their financial troubles. The weight of his family's struggles pressed down on him, threatening to crush his carefully laid plans.

C. GROOMS & BOBBY MAY

"Maya, I'm so sorry," Elijah said, his voice thick with emotion. "But you can't turn to crime. That only makes things worse."

"I know," Maya replied, fear evident in her voice. "I'm just... I'm scared, Elijah. I don't know what's going to happen."

Determination surged through Elijah. "We'll get through this," he promised. "I'll do everything I can to help."

"But what about your basketball career?" Maya asked, her voice trembling. "I don't want to be a burden."

"You're not a burden," Elijah said firmly. "You're my sister, and I love you. Basketball is important, but family comes first. Always."

As he ended the call, Elijah felt the weight of responsibility settle on his shoulders. He had to step

FOR THE LOVE OF THE GAME

up for his family, even if it meant putting his own dreams on hold.

Meanwhile, Clifford grappled with a problem of a different sort. His long-distance relationship with Aliyah was showing signs of strain, the miles between them and the demands of college basketball taking their toll.

"I miss you, Cliff," Aliyah's voice came through the phone, heavy with longing. "It's so hard being apart like this."

Clifford closed his eyes, feeling the ache of separation. "I miss you too," he replied, emotionally. "But we knew this would be tough when I came to Georgetown University ."

"I know," Aliyah said, a note of sadness creeping into her voice. "It just feels like you're slipping away. Like basketball is more important than me. I'm not trying to be selfish. I'm really not but I also need companionship."

C. GROOMS & BOBBY MAY

Guilt washed over Clifford. He knew he had been neglecting their relationship, his focus narrowing to the court and his studies. "I'm sorry, Aliyah," he said softly. "You're one of the most important things to me. Basketball is big and although it's not everything, I definitely need it to keep going. Do you understand that?"

"I do understand that but why does it feel like it is?" Aliyah asked, her voice wavering. "Why does it feel like you're always too busy for me? If I'm so important then you should be available for me too."

Clifford took a deep breath and gathered himself. "Aliyah, I love you. I haven't been the best boyfriend lately, but I promise I'll do better. You're too important to lose."

"Do you really mean that?" Aliyah asked, a glimmer of hope in her voice.

"I do," Clifford affirmed. "I'm not letting basketball come between us. I'll find a way to make this work."

FOR THE LOVE OF THE GAME

As he ended the call, Clifford felt a renewed sense of determination. He had to find a way to balance his commitment to basketball and school with his relationship. All three are integral parts of his life, and he refused to sacrifice one for the other.

The next day, Malik, Elijah, and Clifford met before practice, the weight of their personal struggles evident in their subdued demeanors.

"You, okay?" Malik asked Elijah, concern etched on his face.

Elijah sighed, rubbing his head.
"Not really. My sister got arrested for shoplifting, my family is struggling financially, and I don't know how to help them and keep up with basketball."

Malik's eyes widened in shock. "Man, I'm so sorry. Is she okay?"

"She's scared," Elijah replied. "And so am I, to be honest."

C. GROOMS & BOBBY MAY

Clifford placed a comforting hand on Elijah's shoulder. "We're here for you, no matter what. Whatever you need, just say the word."

Elijah managed a small smile. "Thanks, guys. I don't know what I'd do without both of you."

Malik turned to Clifford, noticing the troubled look on his face. "What about you, Cliff? You look like you've got something on your mind too."

Clifford nodded, his expression pained. "It's Aliyah. We're struggling with the distance. I need to find a way to balance basketball and our relationship better."

"I hear that," Malik said, nodding in understanding. "Juggling everything is tough, but you have to make time for the people who matter."

"You're right," Clifford agreed, a look of determination crossing his face. "I'm trying to make it work and I want to but right now there are only so many hours in a day. Basketball related activities, schoolwork, occasional down time, and sleep take up the rest. I would be lying if I said the pressure I'm feeling isn't weighing on me."

As they headed to practice, the trio felt a sense of unity in the face of their struggles. They knew the road ahead would be tough, but they also knew they had each other to lean on. Sometimes that might be enough, but this felt different.

The next few weeks flew by in a blur of practices, games, and personal struggles. Malik found himself constantly battling his growing feelings for Jasmine, torn between his heart and his commitment to basketball. Elijah worked tirelessly to support his family while maintaining his focus on the court. Clifford made a concerted effort to be a better boyfriend to Aliyah, carving out time for phone calls and video chats amidst his busy schedule.

Then, just as it seemed the weight of their struggles might overwhelm them, a ray of hope broke through.

Elijah's phone rang, his mother's voice brimming with emotion as she delivered the news:

"Elijah, your sister's charges were dropped. The store owner decided not to press charges."

Relief washed over Elijah in a powerful wave. "That's incredible, Mom. How did this happen?"

"It's a miracle," his mother replied, joy evident in her voice. "The store owner knows Maya is a good kid and he also is moved by how much you've been doing to help the family by traveling back and forth from D.C. as much as you have in the past three weeks.

Tears pricked at Elijah's eyes. "I love you, Mom. I love you all so much."

As soon as he ended the call, Elijah rushed to find Malik and Clifford, his heart was light for the first time in weeks. When he shared the news, his friends enveloped him in a celebratory group hug.

FOR THE LOVE OF THE GAME

"That's amazing, E," Malik said, grinning from ear to ear. "I'm so happy for you and your family."

Clifford nodded in agreement. "You stepped up when your family needed you most. You're a true hero, man."

Elijah felt the warmth spread through his chest and gratitude overwhelmed him.
"I couldn't have done it without you guys," he said, his voice thick with emotion. "You've been there for me every step of the way."

Malik slung an arm around Elijah's shoulders. "That's what brothers do. We'll always be there for each other, no matter what."

As they stood there united in their friendship, Elijah realized that he had something truly special which was a family that loved him, friends who supported him unconditionally, and a passion for basketball that drove him to be his best self. With these pillars of support in his life, he knew he could face anything that came his way.

The bonds of brotherhood that tied Malik, Elijah, and Clifford together had been tested but they had emerged stronger for it. As they walked together towards the gym, ready to pour their hearts into another practice, they carried with them the knowledge that some things in life were more important than basketball and that those very things gave them the strength to excel on the court.

Their journey was far from over, and new challenges undoubtedly lay ahead. But with their unwavering support for one another and their shared passion for the game, Malik, Elijah, and Clifford were ready to face whatever came their way, both on and off the court.

FOR THE LOVE OF THE GAME

Chapter 13: Harmonies & Heartbreaks

The pulsating rhythm of a new track filled the studio as Masterson and PHP worked on their debut album. The air crackled with creative energy, each member contributing their unique talent to the mix. As the playback ended, Masterson felt a surge of pride, marveling at how far they'd come.

But beneath the surface, tension simmered. What began as minor disagreements over creative choices soon escalated into heated debates.

"Yo, Masterson," J-Dawg called out, his brow furrowed. "What happened to the flow we agreed on for the second verse?"

Masterson rubbed his head and sighed, "I know we discussed it, but the original just felt right to me."

J-Dawg's frustration was evident, "We're supposed to be on the same page, and you can't call all of the shots. Right now, I'm having a tough time with your micromanaging. You're testing my patience."

"I'm not trying to take over," Masterson replied defensively. "I just want what's best for the song and sometimes the first take in the booth is the realest version. You have to trust me Dawg."

Their producer, Dre,, sensing the rising tension, intervened. "Let's take a break guys, cool off, and come back with fresh ears and mind. We've been working extremely hard on this project and we're almost at the finish line."

As the group filed out of the studio, Masterson couldn't shake the feeling that the bond they'd once shared was recently starting to fray. He struggled to figure out the issue, but he knew that whatever it was could just be in the moment. The group had been putting in long hours for the past three weeks. He shrugged his shoulders and chalked it up to being around each other more than usual. Even the best relationships can be tested simply by being a pain in

FOR THE LOVE OF THE GAME

the ass all the time. Sometimes people just need a break.

Meanwhile, across town, Malik grappled with his own internal conflict. His relationship with Jasmine had deepened, leaving him torn between his growing feelings and his unwavering commitment to basketball.

After a particularly distracting practice session, Elijah pulled Malik aside. "Where's your head at, man? You've been off your game lately. Where's your energy? Your goal is to make it to the league, but I can tell you right now that you're just going through the motions out there. That's not going to cut it."

Malik tried to brush it off. "Just tired, I guess. Sometimes it's like that man. Cut me a little slack."

Elijah, knowing his friend better than that, pressed further. "Come on, Malik. I know you. What's really going on? What's good with you?"

C. GROOMS & BOBBY MAY

Finally, Malik admitted the truth. "It's Jasmine. I really like her, but I'm scared it'll interfere with basketball."

Elijah's expression and stance softened. "It's a tough balance, but you can't let fear hold you back. You might be surprised at how well you can manage both. Is she putting pressure on you or is it you? I'm only asking because one is a minor problem that can be worked out and the other is a full-blown distraction. Either way, this is not the time to go down the rabbit hole of what ifs and mind reading. If you think it's an issue, then talk to Jasmine about it. If not, then I need you to get your mind right and stop creating problems that aren't there at the moment."

As Malik wrestled with matters of the heart, Elijah was emotionally spirally out of control. Since his sister's arrest, he'd been working tirelessly to support his family, often at the expense of his own well-being.

Clifford, noticing the toll it was taking, confronted him. "Elijah, you look exhausted. When's the last time

FOR THE LOVE OF THE GAME

you got a good night's rest? You're sleepwalking out there in a fog."

Elijah shrugged, dark circles prominent under his eyes. "Six hours is a luxury these days but most nights I get about 4 to 5 hours of actual sleep. I'm just trying to be there for my family during a tough stretch and although they keep telling me that things are under control, I just want to show and prove that I'm here if they need me."

"Listen, I feel where you're coming from and it's a good place, but you can't keep this up, Clifford warned. "Burn out is inevitable because this pace is not sustainable. Look man, I get being there for your family, but you need to take care of yourself too."

Despite his friend's concern, Elijah still felt pulled in too many directions, unsure how to balance his family obligations with his own needs and aspirations. This was truly a rough patch for him and for those in his inner circle.

C. GROOMS & BOBBY MAY

Back in the studio, the tension within PHP continued to build. Masterson found himself increasingly at odds with his groupmates, their creative differences threatening to tear them apart.

During a rare moment alone on the phone with Malik, Masterson confided his fears. "I don't know how much longer I can do this. It feels like we're not even on the same page anymore."

Malik, drawing from his own experiences, offered advice. "You have to fight for what you believe in, even when it's hard. But remember, compromise doesn't mean giving up your vision."

Masterson nodded, grateful for his brother's support. "You're right. It's just not easy."

"You're not alone in this, Malik reassured him. You've got people who love you and believe in you, including me." The end of that call was one of resolution and just the right message of inspiration that a younger brother needs from his older sibling. The kind of love

FOR THE LOVE OF THE GAME

and messaging that resonates and lets your brother know that what they are doing is not going unnoticed. Sometimes that's all a person needs to push them over the latest hurdle that life throws at them.

PHP's debut single was gaining traction, and their name was beginning to ring bells. However, each day that passed, Masterson felt a growing sense of responsibility. He wanted their platform to stand for more than just personal success, glamour, and glitz.

He called a meeting with the group to share his vision. "I want us to use our music to make a real difference, to speak out against injustice. We know the industry is full of artists who like to floss their perception of what they think being rich is, but we need to be more than that. I'm all in it for the culture, but let's not lose focus on what's more important, and that's making an impact."

Dre, ever the pragmatist cautioned, "We need to be careful not to alienate our fans. It's a delicate balance."

C. GROOMS & BOBBY MAY

But Masterson held his ground and stood on his square, "We have a responsibility to use our voice for more than just talking about money, hoes, and clothes. There's way more in this culture than just that."

J-Dawg, after a moment of consideration, backed him up. "I'm with you, Masterson. Even if it means taking a risk. I know that I'm on your back a lot and you are damn sure getting on my last nerve, but I believe in your vision." In the background, Dre was looping a sample that he found from Jeane Carne, now that you know how I feel about you, don't let it go to your head no. Now that you know I can't live without you.' That was the genius of Dre, he took a serious situation and not only lightened the mood, but he also expressed the magnitude of the situation and found a sample.

J-Dawg was caught in the moment and chimed in, "what the hell is this that you're listening to?'

FOR THE LOVE OF THE GAME

"Chill, chill, this is the shit. Listen to it with your eyes closed," Dre implored. Masterson was stuck in time between the beat, the lyrics, and the melody. With renewed purpose, PHP was ready to begin incorporating more socially conscious themes into their music. The reaction could be mixed but they were committed and steadfast in their conviction.

Their shows eventually evolved into rallies for change and their music was a powerful call for justice and equality. The sound and message hit Urban America and the suburbs with a powerful impact. Watching his brother's success and commitment to making a difference, Malik felt a surge of inspiration. He knew he had his own battles to fight, both on and off the court, but he also recognized the strength he drew from the love and support of his family and friends.

As this chapter in their lives unfolded, Masterson, Malik, Elijah, and Clifford faced a lot of adversity. However, through it all, they were learning valuable lessons about balance, perseverance, and staying true to oneself. The harmony they sought wasn't just

C. GROOMS & BOBBY MAY

in music or on the basketball court, but in the delicate balance of life itself.

With a deep breath and a renewed sense of purpose, they each faced the road ahead, ready to chase their dreams while holding onto the bonds that kept them grounded. The melody of their futures was still being written, but the rhythm of their shared experiences kept them in sync, even as they navigated their individual paths.

FOR THE LOVE OF THE GAME

Chapter 14: New Beginnings & Bittersweet Endings

The soft morning sunlight seeped through the clouds creating a radiance, over the Georgetown University campus. Malik, Elijah, and Clifford strolled towards the gym breathing in the air in silence. Despite the surroundings, there was an undercurrent of excitement that pulsed through them as they looked forward to what awaited them.

Upon entering the locker room their attention was immediately captured by a face among the coaching staff. A tall and lean man with short hair and sharp eyes stood with authority and confidence exuding from his crossed arms and posture.

Coach Thompson interrupted the silence with a throat clearing before introducing the team to the new addition to the staff, Assistant Coach Rick Peterson. He came from the University of Arizona with a track record of leading teams to conference championship games and deep tournament runs. Coach Peterson acknowledged his introduction by addressing the players with gratitude for joining such a group of athletes.

"I look forward to getting to know each of you and thank you Coach Thompson for giving me the opportunity to contribute to this program. I deeply appreciate it, and I'm honored to be here."

Malik exchanged glances with Elijah and Clifford and then looked around the locker room and saw a mixture of curiosity and unease.

Coach Thompson placed emphasis on teamwork and discipline but also welcoming newcomers as immediate members of the family. From day one, Coach Peterson brought a new dynamic to the mix which was a blend of excitement and intimidation.

"I'm not here to hold your hand " Coach Peterson asserted, his tone firm yet compassionate. "My role is to push you beyond your limits both on and off the court. This involves embracing change, exploring horizons, and stepping out of your comfort zone. My only question to all of you is, are you up for the challenge?" His eyes read the room, and each person nodded their head in unison as a wave of agreement echoed among the team members. Malik had a mix of nerves and anticipation swirling in his gut, but the idea of tackling something new sparked something inside him.

As practice kicked off, it quickly became evident that Coach Peterson's coaching style was different from their past experiences. He leaned heavily on team building by enhancing each player's individual skills and helping them understand the power of synergy.

"Malik," he called out while tossing a basketball his way, "focus on improving your ball handling skills. You need to be able to create scoring opportunities off the dribble. Show me what you can do."

Malik gripped the ball feeling its weight in his palms. He started dribbling, concentrating on the rhythm and precision of each bounce. As he followed Coach Petersons drills, he sensed that his skills could improve by being more fluid and deceptive with his handle but always looking to score.

On the other side of the court, Elijah focused on precision shooting and always moving at game speed. Coach Peterson zoned in on Elijah's mechanics but told him to be more decisive in his actions, "Go harder Elijah and maintain that energy level. Don't shy away from your natural ability. You have what it takes to be a good two-way player."

Elijah cracked a smile with a lot of sweat running down his face, "Thanks Coach. I'll continue putting in the work."

Despite their advancements, moments of tension arose as the team adapted to this new coaching approach. Clifford particularly found it hard to adjust to this contemporary style of hands-on coaching.

"Why are we dedicating time to individual drills?" Clifford questioned Malik during a break for water.

FOR THE LOVE OF THE GAME

His frustration was evident in his tone. "Shouldn't we be focusing on our team offense for the next game?"

Malik took a sip before responding, "I realize it's a bit unconventional, but I can see what he's doing. Just give this approach a shot, Cliff."

Clifford reluctantly agreed, displaying his doubt, but he was also willing to trust the process. Over time, the team started to see the results of their work. Malik's ball handling skills saw an improvement enabling him to create scoring chances where he previously would have passed the ball. Elijah's defense grew formidable causing frustration, for the skilled adversaries. Even Clifford, who initially resisted the techniques, discovered himself excelling under Coach Peterson's mentorship by channeling his frustration into determination on the basketball court.

Despite their progress on the court life, off of the court continued to bring unforeseen issues their way.

C. GROOMS & BOBBY MAY

Clifford faced a crisis due to his long-distance relationship with Aliyah.

"I'm not sure how much longer I can keep this up Cliff "Aliyah admitted during one of their infrequent phone conversations. "Our time together is scarce, and it feels distant when we do meet."

Clifford felt a pang in his heart upon hearing her distress. "I love you Aliyah. I'm committed to making things work." Aliyah took a moment before responding to her voice filled with emotion. "I feel the same way about you but love alone might not be enough right now. It's crucial for us to focus on our paths and aspirations. Maybe it's time to acknowledge that we're moving in directions."

Clifford was deeply affected by her words, and it left him feeling down and broken. In the following days, he mechanically went through his basketball practice routine, his body operating on autopilot while his mind grappled with his heartache. His teammates sensed that something was off but

FOR THE LOVE OF THE GAME

respected his need for solitude and they offered their support through glances and comforting words of reassurance.

"Cliff, you know we're here for you if you ever want to talk " Malik expressed one afternoon after practice with a genuine concern evident in his tone. "We've got your back no matter what."

Clifford nodded appreciatively at the gesture even though he wasn't quite ready to open up. For now, he sought refuge in basketball, finding comfort in the cadence of the game. The love of the game tends to do that sometimes. There's this unspoken peace that settles the mind down and helps you put things in its proper perspective. The rhythmic snapping of the net runs through you like the snare in your favorite hip hop track. You move around on the court with an innate movement blowing past imaginary defenders and going into your pull up jump shot. Every now and then you go to the free throw to settle down and hear your heart beat. It's a place of refuge unlike anything else. When you hit that zone, there is nothing that you cannot do even as the world turns the turmoil of the day into your direction.

With time passing and days turning into weeks, Clifford gradually started to mend. The ache of parting ways with Aliyah didn't vanish entirely but it became more bearable over time.

He poured his emotions into his performance and stepped up as a leader on the court. His newfound focus and drive motivated his teammates and propelling them to new heights.

Meanwhile across the country, Masterson and his group PHP were gearing up for another show. The atmosphere backstage crackled with energy as they prepared to open for the RUN DMC.

"This is our moment " J Dawg exclaimed, excitement gleaming in his eyes. "This is our time to shine." He practiced his lyrics in his head moving around backstage with the type of energy that couldn't be controlled. The rest of the members started doing the same thing. It was poetry in motion at its finest.

Masterson felt a mix of nerves and anticipation rush through him. As they stepped onto the stage and felt the cheers from the crowd washing over them, he understood that this performance was more than about music; it was about spreading a message and using their platform to advocate for change and move the crowd at the same time.

Through his lyrics, Masterson poured out stories about the struggles of his community and the importance of standing up for one's convictions. The audience responded with enthusiasm and their energy fueled his delivery.

After their set concluded Masterson and his crew were elated beyond words. As they went backstage, a man in a suit approached them.

"Hello " he greeted, shaking all of their hands. "I'm Cutty from Universal Records. Your show tonight was amazing. You have the potential to make it big in the hip hop scene. I'd like to discuss the possibility of signing your group to our label."

Masterson felt a rush of excitement and as he looked at his crew, he could see joy and hope reflected in their expressions. "Count us in " he declared, firmly shaking the man's hand. "Let's make it happen."

As they were moving through the venue that evening, PHP sensed they were on the brink of something big. The immediate future seemed bright and full of opportunity. They were built for this very moment though and recognized the gravity of the situation.

Hip Hop was changing in real time with no clear direction, and they were right at the forefront. Their chance to make an immediate impact was coming and there was no looking back.

RUN DMC came to the stage moving to the beat created by the scratching of the record by DJ Jam Master J and RUN yelled into the mic, "HOW YALL

FOR THE LOVE OF THE GAME

FEEL OUT THERE!?" The crowd went wild, and a symphony of sounds shook the floor beneath everybody's feet.

DMC, right in sync as he always seemed to be, chimed in " Aw yeah check this out. One, two, three in the place to be, as it is plain to see, he is DJ RUN and I'm DMC."

PHP found space in the back of the venue to watch stage mastery at its finest. The icons at the top of the game were blessing the stage and it was poetry in motion indeed.

Back on campus, Coach Peterson continued to contribute to the success of the program. The initial pushback phase against his strategies was over and the team found a renewed sense of purpose and camaraderie. Coach Thompson was the ultimate leader, and he knew how to put everything together. As they geared up for the next game, there was a buzz of anticipation in the air. Georgetown University was becoming Black America's team. Every game must

C. GROOMS & BOBBY MAY

see, and the city was buzzing too. In order to understand the dynamics, all you had to do was take a walk around the campus. What becomes plain to see is that the ethnicity of the players on the team did not reflect the actual demographic makeup of the school. However, when a team is winning games, reality tends to get blurred.

The gym noise was at a deafening level as Malik, Elijah, and Clifford glided onto the court leading the team out to warm up. They moved with a different type of harmony and sync. They carried the pride of the hoods that they had come from on their backs but moved around seamlessly and gracefully.

After wrapping up warmups, Coach Thompson called the team together. "I am truly proud of each and every one of you," his voice tinged with emotion. "You've encountered obstacles both on and off the court. You've met them head on too. I want you to remember this; you're not just representing yourselves or the team. You're playing for all those who believed in you and for all those who have supported you on this

FOR THE LOVE OF THE GAME

journey. So go out there and show the world what Georgetown University basketball truly stands for."

C. GROOMS & BOBBY MAY

Chapter 15: Love, Loyalty, & Last Chances

The warm colors of the setting sun cast a light over Georgetown University as Malik and Jasmine sat together on a bench. The campus was peaceful in the evening and Malik's mind was preoccupied with thoughts of his future.

Jasmine leaned in close to him offering both comfort and empathy. "What's weighing on you?" she inquired softly in a gentle tone. "Lately, you've been looking like you're carrying the weight of the world on your shoulders. What's going on? I'm here for you?"

Taking a breath Malik tried to gather his thoughts. "I feel torn Jas. It's like I'm being pulled in too many directions. Some days I feel like everything is going how it's supposed to be and then I get bombarded with stuff. School, practice, back home stuff, my dreams of making it to the league, and keeping our relationship intact. I get overwhelmed sometimes and some days are tough." Malik paused for a second.

FOR THE LOVE OF THE GAME

In the near distance, a car stereo was playing a soulful hook, "I wanna be free shoop shoop shoop.'

"What's eating at you for real? Talk to me" Jasmine probed and snapped him out of his trance.

"My aspirations for the NBA and us. I don't have much of a life beyond basketball and although I understand the work that's involved to make it, the sacrifice is absolutely taking a toll." Malik confessed quietly.

Concern creased Jasmine's forehead as she sat upright. "Why do you believe you can't have both?"

Malik shook his head with frustration evident in his voice. "To succeed in the league I need to be committed. There's very little room for distractions or anything that might disrupt my focus."

A pause lingered between them before Jasmine broke the silence speaking thoughtfully. "Malik you're more than a basketball player. You have aspirations and passion that reach beyond the court. Do you believe

C. GROOMS & BOBBY MAY

that embracing your life could enhance your skills on the court and off?"

Malik felt a lump in his throat. "I'm afraid Jas. Afraid of losing myself and of losing everything that I've worked so hard for."

Jasmine gently held his face in her hands, her touch comforting him. "You won't lose yourself. You're resilient. Your dreams will always be a part of you. Life is more than pursuing one goal. It's about living in the present and treasuring what truly matters."

A tear rolled down Malik's cheek. "I don't know what I did to have you in my life Jas but I'm definitely thankful to have you."

Jasmine's smile was gentle, and her eyes were filled with emotion. "I'm grateful for you too Malik. I'll always stand by your side and love you unconditionally, no matter where your dreams lead us. We're in this journey together." Malik embraced her tightly taking in the fragrance of her hair. With

FOR THE LOVE OF THE GAME

Jasmine by his side he felt prepared to confront any obstacles that came his way.

Meanwhile across town Elijah grappled with the burden of his sister Maya's issues. It weighed heavily on him as he sat in the living room of their family home. His mother's worried eyes focused on him.

"I'm not sure how much more of this I can handle " Elijah admitted, his voice strained. "It seems like every step forward results in two steps backwards. How do we keep moving forward?"

His mother reached out and held his hand reassuringly, "Maya needs us now more than ever and we can't abandon her. You've been coming back and forth from school so much, but we have things under control at the moment. Think about yourself for a moment and this opportunity that you have. Georgetown University is a great school, and I trust Coach Thompson."

C. GROOMS & BOBBY MAY

Elijah nodded with determination despite feeling worn out. "You're right. I'll do everything in my power to ensure she receives the support she requires from a distance. We're a family and families stick together."

However, as Elijah dedicated himself to helping his sister, his commitment to the team began to waver. After missing another practice, Coach Thompson decided to have a talk with Elijah.

"Elijah it's important for you to attend practice " the coach kindly advised. "The team relies on you. We're entering a phase of the season."

Elijah felt a sense of responsibility weighing on him. "I understand, Coach. I'm doing my best to juggle everything, but my family also depends on me."

Coach Thompson's demeanor softened as he replied "I know you're facing difficulties. Just remember that you have support around you. Your teammates, coaches and friends are all here to help. Don't bear the burden alone."

Touched by the coach's empathy Elijah felt a lump in his throat. He expressed his gratitude, "Thank you much for your understanding and support. I really appreciate the lengths that you and the staff have gone to in order to help me mature into a young man. Coming from where I come from, there are so many road blocks to hurdle, betrayal, false promises, and in the midst of all of this there are glimpses of hope. I'm learning to embrace kind gestures with no strings attached but it's not easy coach. I just want you to understand that I am struggling with how to deal with it all and basketball is the only place right now that brings me solace. I truly thank you."

Coach Thompson gave a warm supportive smile and reached out to give Elijah a strong embrace and said "Elijah I'm more than just your basketball coach; I'm your guardian away from home. It's my honor and privilege to hold you accountable as I would my own children. I'll always be here for you even after you graduate." It was at that moment that their bond became solidified.

With a game approaching that would determine their playoff prospects, anxiety grew within the team. Coach Peterson called them together in the locker room to ease some of those fears.

"This is our moment," he asserted with conviction in his voice. "Our season hinges on this game and it's the culmination of what we've been trying to achieve all season. Are we ready to display the essence of what Georgetown University basketball is all about?"

The room echoed with a chorus of agreements. Malik felt a rush of both excitement and nerves. "We've got this!" he reassured himself and his teammates. "It's our time to shine so let's ball out!"

The game was competitive from the start and the lead changed hands back and forth throughout. Malik was playing with precision, but thoughts of Jasmine and his future kept distracting him.

FOR THE LOVE OF THE GAME

During a break in the game Malik turned to Elijah with his voice tinged with urgency. "E, how do you manage it all? How do you find balance?"

Elijah pondered for a moment before responding. "You need to prioritize what truly matters and listen to your heart. Ultimately you're the one living with your decisions."

Malik nodded, though uncertainty lingered in his eyes. ". What if I'm afraid of making the choice?" Sometimes in the game of basketball, and in life, it's these types of random conversations that bring clarity to intense situations and allow us to think things through on the fly.

Elijah placed a reassuring hand on Maliks shoulder meeting his gaze firmly. "Bro, just have faith in those who care for you and stand by you. Sometimes people see qualities in you that you don't notice."

As the decisive moments dwindled down Georgetown University held onto a lead. The

C. GROOMS & BOBBY MAY

spectators rose to their feet creating a deafening roar of noise. When the buzzer sounded, Malik felt a rush of energy over him. However amidst his celebration with his teammates Malik understood that this was just the start. The true tests awaited them.

In the ensuing weeks, Malik strived to juggle his devotion to basketball with his growing bond with Jasmine. One night as they gazed at the stars while lying on a blanket Jasmine turned towards him with her eyes gleaming.

"I'm incredibly proud of you Malik " she whispered softly. "You are my strength and my stability. I need you to know that." Malik kissed her tenderly feeling a wave of tranquility engulf him. He realized he had found love and that his feelings for Jasmine were real.

During a practice leading up to the NCAA tournament, Malik landed awkwardly after grabbing a rebound and twisted his ankle. The pain hit him instantly and intensely. He knew right away this was not a mild sprain. Fatigue has a way of catching up with you, even when you think things are under control. The body is funny like that, one day you're at full strength and in a moment, it's shutting you down.

The following weeks were a mix of rehabilitation and frustration, but through it all, Jasmine stood by his side. She had a way of uplifting his spirits and urging him to persevere when he felt like giving up.

"You're the person I've ever known " she reassured him during a strenuous therapy session. "You'll bounce back from this stronger than ever. I have faith in you."

Her words became Malik's guiding light propelling him onward during his difficult moments. As he gradually recovered his strength and mobility, Malik was aware that tough decisions lay ahead. After lengthy discussions with Jasmine and his family, the time had come. He requested a meeting with Coach Thompson and Coach Peterson. At the meeting, his heart was racing as he stepped into their office, and he summoned up the strength to express his feelings of why he was there to meet them in the first place.

"I'm going to enter the draft after the season is over," he announced calmly despite his nerves. "I need your support, and I can't do it alone. I've had some time to reflect on my experience here at Georgetown University and feel like it's time for me to take it to the next level."

Coach Thompson rose from his seat and placed a hand on Maliks shoulder. His eyes reflected a blend of pride and sorrow. "We're here to support you Malik and you're a part of our family. As you move forward on your journey, always remember that my door will always be open to you."

Tears welled up in Malik's eyes as he felt the warmth of the support. "Thanks, Coach. I appreciate that."

Leaving the office, Malik sensed a burden lifting off his shoulders. The road ahead seemed daunting, but with his team, family, and Jasmine by his side he felt

FOR THE LOVE OF THE GAME

equipped to tackle whatever lay ahead. That evening standing on the balcony of his dorm room with a view of the campus that had been his haven for years, Malik was overcome by a mix of fear, excitement, gratitude, and determination. He thought about Elijahs unwavering dedication to supporting his family while pursuing his aspiration, Clifford's growing passion for journalism that matched his love for basketball, and about Masterson and PHP making waves in the music scene. From their humble beginnings growing up in the concrete jungle to where they stood now, each of them had carved their own path but would forever be connected by unbreakable bonds. Malik silently made a promise to himself that he would help those who had his back and got him to this point in his life. Above all, he vowed never to forget his roots and the individuals who had influenced him on his journey towards self-discovery. As he drifted off to sleep, his dreams were filled with memories of basketball shoes squeaking on hardwood floors, the applause of fans, and the beloved faces of those closest to him. For the first time in an exceptionally long time, he was happy.

C. GROOMS & BOBBY MAY

Chapter 16: Decisions & Departure

The crisp autumn air of New York City filled Masterson's lungs as he stepped out of the sleek elevator onto the top floor of a towering skyscraper. His heart raced with a mixture of excitement and apprehension as he was ushered into a plush office, the Manhattan skyline sprawling out behind floor-to-ceiling windows.

Across a polished mahogany table sat three executives from Warner Brothers, their tailored suits and practiced smiles exuding an air of power and promise. The head executive, a silver-haired man with piercing blue eyes, leaned forward, his voice smooth as silk.

"Masterson, we're prepared to offer PHP a deal that will change your lives," he said, sliding a document across the table. "We're talking about a multimillion-dollar contract, the best producers, a top-tier marketing team, and everything you need to take your

FOR THE LOVE OF THE GAME

music to the next level. All you have to do is sign on the dotted line."

Masterson's fingers tingled as he reached for the contract, the weight of the moment not lost on him. This was what he had dreamed of since he first picked up a microphone in his cramped bedroom in Harlem. This was his chance to share his music with the world and make a real impact. Yet, as his eyes scanned the document, a nagging feeling tugged at the back of his mind. The executives watched him with calculating eyes, their smiles never quite reaching their eyes. Masterson cleared his throat, choosing his words carefully.

"I appreciate the offer," he said, setting the contract back on the table. "But this is a big decision, one that affects not just me, but my whole crew. I need time to think it over and discuss it with them. I hope you understand."

The head executive's smile faltered for a fraction of a second before returning, wider than ever. "Of course,

Masterson. We completely understand. Take all the time you need to consider our offer. But remember, opportunities like this are rare in this industry so don't take too long."

As Masterson left the office and descended to the bustling streets below, the weight of the decision pressed down on him. He pulled out his phone, his fingers hovering over J-Dawg's number for a moment before he made the call.

"Yo, Masterson!" J-Dawg's voice crackled through the speaker, the sounds of laughter and music in the background. "How'd the meeting go? Did they offer us a deal?"

Masterson took a deep breath, leaning against the cool stone of a nearby building. "Yeah, they did. It's big, J. Bigger than we ever imagined. But..."

"But what?" J-Dawg's tone sharpened. "This is what we've been working for, isn't it? What's the problem?"

FOR THE LOVE OF THE GAME

"I don't know, man," Masterson sighed, rubbing his head. "Something about these guys just doesn't feel right. It's like they're not in it for the music, you know? Like we're just another product to them."

There was a long pause on the other end of the line. When J-Dawg spoke again, his voice was quieter, more thoughtful. "I hear you, Mass. But we've got to think about the big picture here. This could be our shot, our chance to make it big. We can't just turn it down because of a feeling, can we?"

Masterson closed his eyes, conflict raging within him. "I know, J. I know. But we've come too far to compromise now. We need to do more research, make sure this is the right move for us. I don't want to sign anything until we're absolutely sure."

J-Dawg sighed, but there was understanding in his voice. "Alright, Mass. You're the leader, and I trust your judgment. Just don't take too long, you feel me? We don't want to miss our shot."

C. GROOMS & BOBBY MAY

As Masterson hung up, he felt the weight of responsibility settle on his shoulders. He had a lot of work to do, and he needed his crew by his side. Their future hung in the balance, and he was determined to make the right choice, no matter how difficult it might be. Music industry contracts tend to be filled with ambiguous language that can have the opposite effect of what many artists expect to happen in their lives. One day you're signing a 2 million dollar advance and 5 albums from now, the company is still recouping off of your first album. Masterson heard the stories before but now it was time to hire a lawyer and read the contract thoroughly. Cross collateralization clauses are one of the multiple ways that so many artists ultimately end up losing money, especially for under-performing album sales.

Meanwhile, back in D.C., Clifford found himself grappling with his own set of doubts. As he sat on the bleachers zoned out after practice, Malik approached with concern etched on his face.

FOR THE LOVE OF THE GAME

"You okay, Cliff?" Malik asked, settling down beside his friend. "You've seemed off lately."

Clifford sighed, struggling to put his feelings into words. "I don't know, man. I feel like I'm not sure what I want anymore. Like there's something else out there for me beyond basketball."

Malik nodded, understanding in his eyes. "It's not easy figuring out what you want to do with your life. But you've got options, Cliff. You're not just a basketball player. You've got talents and passions that go way beyond the court."

Clifford turned to his friend, a spark of excitement in his eyes. "I've been thinking about journalism, actually. Writing about sports and telling the stories behind the games. Do you think that's crazy?"

A slow smile spread across Malik's face. "Not at all. I think that's an amazing idea. You've got a gift with words, Cliff, and a unique perspective. You could really make a difference."

C. GROOMS & BOBBY MAY

As they talked, Clifford felt a surge of excitement building within him. Maybe this was what he had been searching for, the missing piece that would make everything fall into place. But even as hope bloomed, doubt crept in.

"I can't just abandon the team, though," he said, his brow furrowing. "We've come so far together."

Malik placed a hand on his shoulder, his grip firm and reassuring. "No one's asking you to abandon anything, Cliff. You give everything you've got to this team for as long as you're here. But there's nothing wrong with thinking about what's next. And no matter what you decide, we've got your back. Always."

Clifford felt a sense of peace wash over him. He knew he had some tough choices ahead, but he also had the unwavering support of his teammates. Whatever path he chose, he wouldn't walk it alone.

As Clifford grappled with his future, the team faced a crisis of its own. Their star player, Marcus, had gone down with what looked to be a season-ending injury. The loss hit the team hard, and as they struggled to adjust, cracks began to show in their once-solid foundation.

"This is a significant setback," Coach Thompson said, his usual confidence tempered by concern. "Marcus was a crucial part of our offense and his absence will be deeply felt."

The team knew they had to step up, but as the losses began to mount, their chemistry frayed. Frustration boiled over and players began pointing fingers, the unity they had worked so hard to build threatening to crumble.

It was Elijah who finally called for a team meeting, his voice cutting through the tension in the locker room. "We need to get it together," he said, his eyes moving from one teammate to another. "We can't keep playing like individuals. We're a team, and it's time we started acting like one."

Malik stood beside him, nodding in agreement. "Elijah's right. We've got to start playing for each other. That's the only way we're going to turn this around."

Their words seemed to strike a chord, and slowly, the team began to rally. They threw themselves into training with renewed vigor, each player pushing themselves and their teammates to be better.

Then, just when it seemed things couldn't get any more intense, Coach Peterson called a meeting. The team gathered, curiosity and apprehension mingling in the air.

"I've been talking to the doctors," Coach Peterson said, a glimmer of hope in his eyes. "There's a chance, a small one but a chance nonetheless, that Marcus could come back this season. If he works hard in his rehabilitation, he might be able to join us just in time for the NCAA tournament."

FOR THE LOVE OF THE GAME

The news was met with a mix of excitement and disbelief. They knew it was a long shot, but the mere possibility of Marcus's return ignited a fire within the team. They threw themselves into their training with renewed energy, determined to be ready if and when their teammate returned.

Malik and Elijah stepped up, taking on leadership roles both on and off the court. They organized extra practice sessions, worked one-on-one with struggling teammates, and fostered a sense of unity and purpose that had been missing since Marcus's injury.

Slowly but surely, the team began to come back together. Wins that had once seemed impossible became a reality. They played with a joy and camaraderie that had been absent for too long, each victory bringing them closer as a team and as friends.

Then, on a cool evening in early March, as the team warmed up for their game, a familiar figure appeared at the entrance to the court. Marcus, dressed in his

C. GROOMS & BOBBY MAY

uniform, stepped onto the hardwood to a deafening roar from the crowd. His teammates rushed to embrace him, the emotions of the moment overwhelming them all. Malik reached him first, pulling his friend into a tight hug.

"Welcome back," Malik said, his voice thick with emotion. "We missed you, man."

Marcus grinned, his eyes shining with unshed tears. "It's good to be back. There were times I wasn't sure if I'd make it, but I couldn't let you guys down."

That night, the team played as if they were possessed. Their passes were crisp, and their shots were falling as if guided by an unseen hand. Malik and Elijah were unstoppable, their on-court chemistry on full display. And Marcus, coming off the bench, provided the spark that pushed them over the edge.

When the final buzzer sounded, the scoreboard showed a decisive victory. The team rushed onto the

FOR THE LOVE OF THE GAME

court, their celebration a release of weeks of pent-up emotion and hard work.

As they stood together, arms around each other, they knew they had something special. They had faced their doubts and fears head-on and emerged stronger for it. They were more than just a team now; they were a family bound together by shared struggle and triumph.

In that moment, as the crowd's cheers washed over them, they felt invincible. They had each other, and they had the game they loved. With those two things, nothing seemed impossible. They were champions, not just in name, but in spirit. This was a testament to the power of perseverance, unity, and unwavering belief in oneself and one's teammates.

As they made their way back to the locker room, arms still around each other, they knew that whatever lay ahead, they would face them together. The future was uncertain, but they were ready for it, armed with

C. GROOMS & BOBBY MAY

the strength of their bond and the fire of their shared passion.

For Malik, Elijah, Clifford, and the rest of the team this was more than just a victory, it was an affirmation of everything they had worked for and everything they believed in. It was a moment that would stay with them long after their playing days were over, a reminder of what could be achieved when a group of individuals came together as one and united in pursuit of a common goal.

As they celebrated into the night with their laughter and joy echoing through the campus, they knew that this was just the beginning. The road ahead would be long but they were ready to face it together head on.

FOR THE LOVE OF THE GAME

Chapter 17: Rainy Days

A relentless downpour battered Georgetown University's campus, mirroring the turmoil in Elijah's heart. He sat on his bed, the rhythmic patter of rain against his dorm window providing a somber backdrop to his thoughts. Weeks had passed since his sister Maya's latest arrest and the situation had escalated beyond anything he could have imagined.

His phone buzzed, cutting through the sound of the rain. His mother's name flashed on the screen, and Elijah's heart sank as he answered.

"Elijah," his mother's voice cracked with emotion. "I need you to come home. It's Maya. She's in real trouble this time."

"What happened?" Elijah asked, dread settling in his stomach.

"They're talking about prison, Elijah. She's being charged with possession with intent to sell."

C. GROOMS & BOBBY MAY

The words hit Elijah like a physical blow. As the rain intensified outside, he knew he had to be there for his family even if it meant leaving his team during the season's most critical moment. He began to pack, his mind racing with thoughts of Malik, Clifford, and his coaches and all who had believed in him. But family had to come first.

Across town, Malik stood by a rain-streaked window, facing his own storm of his own. His relationship with Jasmine had deepened but so had the tension between his love for her and his commitment to basketball.

"I don't know how much longer I can do this, Malik," Jasmine confessed, her voice was barely audible above the rain. "I feel like I'm always second to basketball."

Guilt pierced Malik's heart. He knew she was right. "I'm sorry, Jas," he said softly. "I promise to make it up to you. I'll balance everything better and make sure you always come first."

FOR THE LOVE OF THE GAME

Jasmine searched his face. "Do you mean that?"

Malik met her gaze, taking a deep breath. "I'm in this for the long haul, Jas. From now on, you're my number one priority."

Jasmine's smile was tinged with relief as she hugged him tightly. As they stood there, the rain creating a cocoon around them, Malik felt a sense of peace wash over him. He knew balancing his love for Jasmine with basketball would be tough, but he was ready to weather this storm.

Meanwhile, Masterson and his crew, PHP, found themselves in the midst of their own turmoil. They grappled with the consequences of their record label deal with Warner Brothers Records, working tirelessly on their debut album as the label pushed them to change their sound to fit current trends.

C. GROOMS & BOBBY MAY

"I feel like we're losing ourselves," J-Dawg confided to Masterson, the sound of the downpour a constant presence.

Masterson nodded grimly. "But what can we do? We signed a contract. Damn, I knew they had that look in their eyes in that meeting, but it was hard to turn down 70 million."

J-Dawg's eyes lit up with a spark of determination. "Maybe we can find a way out without losing everything."

Hope surged through Masterson, like a ray of sunlight breaking through storm clouds. It was a long shot, but they had to try. Over the next few days, as the rain continued unabated, they went over the contract, consulted lawyers, and crafted a plan. It was risky, but necessary if they wanted to reclaim their artistic integrity.

Eventually they confronted the label executives, stating their case with unwavering resolve.

FOR THE LOVE OF THE GAME

"We can't keep compromising our values," Masterson declared, his voice steady against the backdrop of thunder. "We got into this to make meaningful music. That's what we're going to do, with or without your support. It seems to me that you know what we bring to the table individually and collectively as a group or you would have never offered us a seven-figure contract. "

The executives, stunned by their determination but mindful of their legal obligations to their artists, eventually agreed to let PHP out of their contract. As Masterson and J-Dawg walked out of the office into the rain-soaked night, elation washed over them. They had weathered this storm and taken a stand for their art and their principles.

A week later, as the rain finally began to subside, PHP signed a new deal with Warner Brothers Records, one that allowed them to maintain creative control over their sound. It was a fresh start and a chance to create the music they had always dreamed of making.

C. GROOMS & BOBBY MAY

As the clouds began to part and Elijah prepared to head back home again, Malik worked on balancing his relationship and his basketball career, and Masterson began to dive back into creating authentic music. Each of them had faced their own personal downpour, but through these trials, they were learning valuable lessons about resilience, integrity, and the importance of staying true to oneself. Their journeys were far from over, and more storms undoubtedly lay ahead. Yet, each of them was determined to face their problems head-on. They had found strength in their families, their relationships, and their passions. As they moved forward, they carried with them the knowledge that they had the courage to dance in the rain, and to stand up for what they believed in even when the skies were at their darkest.

The future remained uncertain for all of them, but the next chapter of their lives were right in front of them. They stood at a crossroads, each facing decisions that would shape their futures. But they faced these moments with the resilience and determination that

FOR THE LOVE OF THE GAME

had brought them this far and confident in their ability to find their way through adversity.

C. GROOMS & BOBBY MAY

Chapter 18: Mass Appeal

The morning sun broke through the clouds as Elijah approached the gym, his heart heavy with the decision he'd made. After days at home, navigating his sister's legal troubles and supporting his family, he'd chosen to return to Georgetown University . He couldn't abandon his team because all of them had stood by him through thick and thin.

As he pushed open the gym doors, he was met with a sight that nearly brought him to tears. The entire team stood waiting, their faces a mix of concern and support.

Malik stepped forward and gave Elijah a tight embrace. "Welcome back, brother. We missed you."

Elijah's voice trembled as he replied, "I missed you guys too. I'm sorry I had to leave, but"

FOR THE LOVE OF THE GAME

"Family comes first," Clifford interjected, squeezing Elijah's shoulder. "We understand. We're just glad you're back."

Coach Thompson's voice rang out, addressing the team. "Elijah, you're an integral part of this family. We're here for you no matter what. I need you to always know that. Now, everybody get on the baseline."

As they began warm-ups, Elijah felt a renewed sense of purpose coursing through him. He attacked each drill with fierce intensity, determined to prove his commitment to the team and their shared dreams.

Meanwhile, Clifford grappled with his own internal struggle. His passion for journalism was growing, threatening to overshadow his love for basketball. After practice, he confided in Malik.

"I don't know what to do," Clifford admitted. "I love this game but there's something else calling me."

C. GROOMS & BOBBY MAY

Malik nodded, understanding in his eyes. "You've got to follow your heart, Cliff. Do what makes you happy." Taking his friend's advice to heart, Clifford began taking small steps towards his newfound passion. He wrote for the school newspaper, covering other teams' games and profiling teammates. He reached out to journalists and editors seeking guidance on breaking into the industry. Unbeknownst to him, Coach Thomspon had also reached out to some of his contacts to help.

Balancing his commitment to the team with his growing love for journalism wasn't easy, but Clifford refused to let his dreams slip away. His articles gained traction, catching the eye of local and even national publications.

As Clifford and Elijah navigated their personal journeys, Malik faced a crisis of his own. His relationship with Jasmine had reached a breaking point because the demands of his basketball career were pulling him in too many directions.

FOR THE LOVE OF THE GAME

"I don't know how much longer I can do this," Jasmine confessed one night, her voice trembling. "I love you, Malik, but again, I feel like I'm always second to basketball."

Guilt washed over Malik as he realized the truth in her words. He had been neglecting her in favor of his NBA dreams. But he couldn't turn his back on his team either. With a heavy heart, Malik expressed his true feelings that he had been carrying for a little while.

"I'm sorry Jasmine but I can't give up on my dreams and basketball is everything to me right now. I've really put in the effort to try and see you more to spend time but I'm getting the feeling that you don't see things from my side when it comes to this. I really care for you, but I need you to decide whether to be all in with me on this journey or you're going to be all out. There are only 24 hours in a day, so I need you to bear with me. October to June are very intense months during this process. If you're struggling right now, how are you going to be if I get drafted, possibly moving to a new city, and on the road constantly?

C. GROOMS & BOBBY MAY

Have you even considered that you might be somewhat selfish in your line of thinking?"

Jasmine's eyes were filled with hurt and disappointment. "I understand what you're saying but I can't be second anymore Malik. Maybe you're right and maybe I'm wrong for feeling this way but I can't ignore my feelings, and you'll probably end up leaving me anyway."

Malik interjected, "This is what I'm talking about. If you were going to really be there for me, then you would see all of the sacrifices that I made to try and make our relationship work. But because you're too focused on yourself, you can't help yourself, right? Look, I know you have some abandonment issues from your father not being in your life on a regular basis after your parents divorced in high school, but every relationship doesn't have to end that way. Your pessimistic ways are becoming a burden too and I don't want to deal with that anymore. I'm sorry but I can't. This is the energy that you put out there and this is what came back. You can never say that I didn't care for you." Jasmine was hurt by the truth that was delivered, and she had not confronted her underlying issues. It didn't matter if Malik spent every hour of the day with her, it simply wasn't going to be enough. Her issue was not with Malik; it was with herself.

Ultimately, she agreed to end their relationship. Malik felt shattered but he knew deep down in his soul that he had made the right decision. However, his performance on the court suffered as he struggled to come to terms with the loss. His shots clanged off the rim, his passes sailed wide. His teammates noticed and there was concern etched on their faces.

"Malik, what's going on?" Elijah asked after a particularly rough practice. "Talk to me, man."

Malik's shoulders slumped as he confessed, "I messed up, Elijah. I let Jasmine walk out of my life. I feel like I'm losing everything that matters. I think I could've stopped her, but I didn't. I couldn't man."
Elijah's grip on Malik's shoulder was firm and reassuring. "You haven't lost anything brother. You've

still got us and the team. We're here for you no matter what. Besides, there are a hundred Jasmines out there and if she couldn't see your effort then she was never going to see it and she wasn't the one for you."

Malik stood there still hurting but relieved that his brother from another mother felt his pain and helped him lift the burden off of his shoulders. As the week passed, Malik's teammates rallied around him. They stayed late after practice, working on his shot and ball handling. They invited him for dinners and movie nights, reminding him of the bonds they shared.

Slowly but surely, Malik began to find his way back. His focus returned and his fire was reignited. He had leaned on his teammates for support, drawing strength from their unwavering belief in him, and they came through for him.

As the tournament loomed in the shadows, Malik, Elijah, and Clifford found themselves pulled in different directions by their individual struggles and aspirations, but their bond pulled them through.

FOR THE LOVE OF THE GAME

Chapter 19 Crossroads & Consequences

The dim overhead lights in the recording studio cast a glow over Masterson, J Dawg and Dre as they gathered around the mixing console. Weariness was evident on their faces, having put in countless hours over the last few days to complete their first album.

"This isn't what we anticipated " J Dawg expressed with frustration in his tone. "Our goal is to create music and not just produce what the record label believes will be profitable."

Dre shook his head with a sense of resignation in his gaze. "We're bound by the contract. If we don't deliver as expected they'll let us go too. We were fortunate to get out of our last contract, so we have to dig a little deeper and make this work."

Masterson massaged his temples attempting to concentrate amidst mounting pressure. "This feels unfamiliar now " he murmured softly. "Our essence and individuality are eroding away."

C. GROOMS & BOBBY MAY

J Dawg's eyes reflected determination, "Then we need to push and keep our integrity even if it compromises sales."

Masterson respected his friends' resolve but he also understood that breaking free from another contract was possible. However, it could bring about repercussions they weren't ready to confront. They had narrowly avoided a lawsuit with Universal Records but now the pressure was mounting with Warner Brothers as well.

"We need to think." Masterson advised, his tone composed yet resolute. "We can't afford to sever all ties. It's crucial to have a plan in place. If we continue on this path, then we risk being labeled troublemakers and ostracized."

The three men deliberated on tactics for hours. They understood the risks of challenging the status quo and were unwilling to compromise their music and message for monetary gain.

FOR THE LOVE OF THE GAME

As dawn approached Masterson felt a surge of determination. "Let's take action " he declared confidently. "We have to create an album that reflects our truth. If the label disapproves, we'll find another path. We are PHP; we answer to no one." J Dawg and Dre nodded in agreement embodying resolve. Their music transcended employment or monetary reward; it was a mission and a means to amplify voices and confront authority, with honesty.

Fueled by this conviction, they channeled their emotions into every melody and lyric. The sounds of The Charmel's track "Long As I've Got You" reverberated through the studio as they embarked on a creative journey. The lyrics resonated with their longing for freedom and authenticity expressing a sense of liberation.

Masterson and PHP found themselves facing difficult challenges as they dared to defy the norms of the industry. While risking it all, they remained steadfast in staying true to their artistry and were determined not to compromise their integrity.

C. GROOMS & BOBBY MAY

Meanwhile in D.C., Elijah grappled with finding his balance both on and off the basketball court. Despite improvements in his family life, his own personal distractions seemed to be affecting his performance on the court.

Following a practice session Malik approached Elijah with concern etched across his face. "What's been bothering you? You seem off your game lately missing shots you'd normally make effortlessly."

Elijah let out a sigh visibly weighed down by his turmoil. "I feel like I'm being pulled in too many directions. It's hard for me to concentrate." Sympathetically nodding, Malik acknowledged the difficulty of juggling responsibilities. "Balancing everything isn't easy but don't forget why you fell in love with basketball in the place. It's about embracing competition and pushing yourself beyond limits." Elijah absorbed the wisdom of his friend's advice realizing that he needed to rediscover his passion and motivation for the love of the game.

FOR THE LOVE OF THE GAME

"Absolutely" he nodded, his voice filled with determination. "I've strayed from the essentials. It's time to refocus and to recall why I started this journey in the first place."

With the end of the tournament approaching, the team's chances of winning it all were hanging in the balance. Throughout the year they had battled through adversity and setbacks, but now every move on the court now carried increased significance.

Coach Thompson gathered his players in the locker room before the game. "This moment " he declared loudly "will define us as individuals."

The players listened intently to understand what was at stake.

"I know you're exhausted and feeling pain " Coach continued. "Within each of you burns a flame that cannot be extinguished. Channel that energy tonight. Give your all on the court."

C. GROOMS & BOBBY MAY

Malik and Elijah exchanged a look. They had confronted their fears before, but now with a championship within reach they knew they had to push themselves more than ever. As they stepped onto the court there was a buzz in the air. Both teams were ready to compete, but Malik and Elijah stood out. They were able to display their talent and determination in every play and scored at will repeatedly. When the final buzzer went off, Georgetown University survived and kept their goal of winning a National Championship alive.

Coach Thompson called Malik and Elijah over and his eyes were gleaming with pride. "You both were outstanding", he remarked, his voice filled with emotion. "The way you played and led; it was truly remarkable. This is the beginning of something special. I need you to bring that same energy from here on out." Malik and Elijah beamed with joy and gratitude. In that moment they felt unbeatable.

FOR THE LOVE OF THE GAME

Chapter 20: One Mic

The recording studio was unusually quiet except for the humming of the air conditioning and occasional chair creaks. Masterson gazed at the mixing board, his tired eyes and shaky hands giving away his fatigue and excitement.

Beside him J Dawg and Dre were bent over their notebooks hastily jotting down tweaks to the lyrics. They had been tirelessly working for weeks to perfect their album. As the release date neared, they understood that the moment of truth had finally come.

Masterson took a breath in an attempt to calm his nerves. This album wasn't a collection of songs; it reflected their identity and values. He knew that not everyone would grasp or embrace their message fully. The record label executives had raised concerns about lyrics cautioning them about potential backlash.

"Hey Masterson," J Dawg chimed in with a smile as he glanced up from his notebook. "You ready for this ride? We're about to make waves and honestly I don't care but people need to get the message."

Masterson nodded solemnly. "I hear you J. We need to brace ourselves for whatever comes our way because it's not going to be smooth sailing for everyone."

Dre leaned back in his chair lost in contemplation. "Indeed, that's the crux of it isn't it? Our goal isn't to please everyone. We're here to express our thoughts authentically and use our platform for those who often go through life unheard."

As the release date for their album drew near, anticipation and excitement surrounding PHP intensified. Music bloggers and media channels were abuzz with chatter about the group's style and controversial lyrics.

FOR THE LOVE OF THE GAME

The actual album launch caused quite a stir in the music scene. Reviews and reactions were polarizing with some praising them as visionaries while others criticized them for being reckless.

Masterson observed these responses with conflicting emotions. They had crafted something that had the potential to spark change and touch lives. However, they found themselves navigating the blurred lines between staying true to their artistry, meeting industry expectations, and dealing with fan reactions.

As opposition mounted, including protests and calls for boycotts from those who believed they had violated societal boundaries, Masterson began questioning their choices.

"I wonder if we pushed things too far", Masterson confided in J one evening with his tone tinged with uncertainty. "Perhaps we should have played it safe."

J Dawg vehemently shook his head. "Nah! Fuck that man. We did what was necessary. We shared our voice; if some can't handle it that's, on them."

In D.C., Elijah felt a sense of determination and focus. Ever since his heart to heart with Malik, he had been putting in an effort to reignite his passion and motivation.

As the team geared up for their next game, Elijah approached each drill and practice with unwavering dedication. Coach Thompson noticed the change in him and gave him a pat on the back after a grueling session. "You're looking sharp out there Elijah. Keep up that energy. We'll be a force to be reckoned."

In the next game, the crowd was on edge with excitement. Right from the start both teams played aggressively exchanging baskets and fighting for every loose ball. As the game progressed, Elijah started to stand out. He effortlessly maneuvered defenders to score time after time and his game was on another level.

FOR THE LOVE OF THE GAME

After celebrating their latest win, Malik pulled Elijah aside with a proud look on his face. "E , I have never seen anybody get busy the way you did tonight. You've been putting in work lately and it's starting to show. Salute to you brother for real."

Elijah was humbled and Malik kept talking excitedly, "NBA scouts have shown major interest in me, and they believe I have a legit shot of going in the first round of the draft." Elijah felt a rush of excitement and pride for his friend, "That's amazing Mal" he expressed sincerely. "You truly deserve this."

However, Malik appeared conflicted and torn between his aspirations and his loyalty. "I'm not sure what to do at this point though. I'd be lying if I said I didn't think about it all the time." he confided softly. "I got word through the grapevine that several teams are showing interest so I'm giving my all out there and doing my best to also not let us down."

Elijah placed a hand on Maliks shoulder. "You could never be a disappointment to us man. You've dedicated everything to this team. This is your dream and it's your time to shine. I'm going all out because I see how hard you've been pushing yourself the last couple of weeks and I'm truly inspired."

Malik shifted the conversation back to Elijah, "If you keep playing like you did tonight, you'll be getting drafted too." They gave each other dap and re-joined the rest of the team. Off in the distance, Coach Thompson smiled at what he had just witnessed.

Even though the future was calling, Malik made a conscious effort to focus on the here and now and focus on winning a championship with Georgetown University. Coach Thompson had been giving him unwavering support after Malik told him that he was going to enter the draft, so Malik was dedicated to keeping that same energy.

FOR THE LOVE OF THE GAME

Chapter 21: Balancing Acts

The Georgetown University Hoyas' locker room was filled with energy after their third consecutive postseason victory. Elijah sat in front of his locker, eyes closed, savoring the moment. He had just played the game of his life and scored a career-high 42 points leading the team to a nail-biting 78-76 win.

Despite the triumph, unease settled in his stomach. The pressure was mounting with each game as the stakes grew higher. Malik plopped down beside him, grinning. "Yo, E, you were on fire again tonight. You keep this up and we'll be cutting down the nets baby!!!"

Elijah forced a smile. "Thanks, Mal. But let's not get ahead of ourselves man." Malik's expression changed slightly. "I know man but one thing that I've learned this season is to learn to live in the moment because anything can happen. You're out there shining and carrying us right now. My draft stock hasn't dropped, and I'm still projected to go in the first round. I know it's not your dream but you're getting looks now too. That's dope to me." As they left the locker room, Elijah fell into step with Clifford, noticing the notebook in his hand. "Working on another story for the school paper?"

Clifford's eyes lit up. "Nah, man. This is for The Washington Post. They want me to write about our team's journey."

Elijah's eyebrows shot up. "The Washington Post? That's huge, Cliff. Congratulations."

Clifford shrugged, a mix of pride and uncertainty on his face. "Thanks, E. But balancing writing with basketball and school is a lot."

Elijah squeezed his friend's shoulder. "You're a talented writer with a gift for storytelling. If anyone can handle this, it's you."

Meanwhile, in the studio, Masterson and PHP grappled with the fallout from their debut album. The

FOR THE LOVE OF THE GAME

controversy surrounding their lyrics had divided critics and fans alike.

J-Dawg was frustrated with it all, "I don't know how much longer I can take this. People are either calling us geniuses or condemning us as irresponsible."

Dre nodded grimly. "We knew this was a risk when we decided to push the envelope. We can't back down now."

Masterson remained silent, his mind racing. They had created something special, something that could inspire change. But they were walking a fine line between artistic integrity, industry demands, and societal pressures. In every city that they performed, a special division of the police, called the Hip Hop Cops, would camp out in their shows. The presence was not about protection; it was to intimidate them from performing their trending single Peace of Mine. It was a socio-political song that addressed police brutality in the urban community and pushing back

C. GROOMS & BOBBY MAY

against the powers that be. The song was popular and sweeping across the nation.

"Maybe we need to reassess," he said finally. "Find a way to push boundaries without alienating everyone."

J-Dawg and Dre exchanged uncertain glances. "What are you saying? You want us to change our sound and our message?"

Masterson shook his head. "Not change. Evolve. We've always spoken truth to power by giving a voice to the voiceless. But maybe we need to find a new way to do that without capitalizing on shock value." J and Dre stood in silence but there was value in what Masterson had to say. "Look, honestly, I didn't expect that song to take off the way that it did and I figured only our die-hard fans would receive it wholeheartedly. The content is definitely relevant so maybe we can use the song as a teaching point in some of the community-based programs and spread the message to our youth."

FOR THE LOVE OF THE GAME

Back in D.C., the Georgetown University Hoyas prepared for their biggest test yet: facing the top-seeded team in the tournament.

Coach Thompson gathered the team in the locker room. "I know you're feeling the pressure. But I also know you're ready for this. You've worked harder than anyone else to get here, and you have the talent and heart to win this game. Welcome to the Final Four gentlemen. It's time to seize the moment."

Malik's expression was fierce. "Coach is right. We've been through too much to let the pressure get to us now. We've got to stay focused, stay united, and play our game." As they took the court, Elijah felt a sense of calm and purpose. This was their moment. The game was a battle from the opening tip with both teams trading baskets and matching intensity levels. The officiating was tight as they attempted to have control of the game. As the minutes ticked down, Elijah struggled. His shots weren't falling, his passes were off, and he was in and out of focus. During a timeout, Coach Thompson pulled him aside.

C. GROOMS & BOBBY MAY

"Elijah, I know you're struggling. But remember who you are. You're one of the best players in the country, and your team needs you. The game comes easy to you so what's going on out there? You don't have to have a career night scoring for us to win, you do know that right?" Elijah loosened up and nodded with a lump in his throat, "Coach, you're right. I'm going to do whatever it takes to help the team and tonight is not just about scoring. I'll hit the glass and dig in on defense. I got you."

Walking back onto the court, he took a deep breath, cleared his mind, and found his rhythm. Ironically, his shots started to fall, and his passes became crisp. The energy of his teammates lifted him up and he dug his heels in on defense and became demonstrative. His energy had changed the course of the game.

When the final buzzer sounded, Georgetown University had pulled off the upset of the tournament. As they celebrated, Coach Thompson stood beside Elijah, his voice thick with emotion. "I

FOR THE LOVE OF THE GAME

knew you had it in you. I've watched you grow over this past year, and I couldn't be prouder son."

Elijah felt a surge of gratitude and love. He owed so much to Coach Thompson, who had believed in him from the start. Looking at his teammates, Elijah knew he was a part of something special. They were a family bound by their love and passion for the game. And with that bond he knew they could achieve anything.

C. GROOMS & BOBBY MAY

Chapter 22: The Final Countdown

The Georgia Dome roared with excitement as the Georgetown University Hoyas faced off against the heavily favored Houston Cougars in the championship game. Malik, Elijah, and Clifford had fought their way here with grit, determination, and a bond that transcended the court.

From the opening tip, both teams brought their A-game. The Cougars had future NBA stars and a stifling defense that seemed to snuff out every Hoyas possession. But Georgetown University refused to back down, matching them blow for blow and playing with a fire that ignited the arena.

Malik scored from every angle with relentless energy, leaving Cougar defenders gasping. Elijah shut down Houston's best players with clutch steals and blocks. Clifford, the team's charismatic leader, dove for loose balls and hit big shots when needed most.

FOR THE LOVE OF THE GAME

As the game wore on, the intensity took its toll. Coach Thompson saw the exhaustion in his players' eyes but also a fierce determination to win. During a timeout, he gathered them around.

"I know you're tired and hurting," he said, his voice hoarse with emotion. "But find something extra, something you didn't know you had. This game is bigger than you and me but don't let the sum total of your existence be eight to ten pounds of air."

Malik, jaw set with determination, replied, "We've come too far to let it slip now."

Elijah's eyes blazed with intensity. "This is our moment. We have to seize it."

Clifford, usually quiet, added, "We're a family. We've been through hell and back together. Nothing can break us now."

The team broke the huddle with a fierce battle cry. They played the final minutes with purpose and unity,

C. GROOMS & BOBBY MAY

leaving the crowd in awe. Malik scored the go-ahead basket with seconds left, and Elijah sealed the victory with a huge block on the Cougars' final possession that fell right into Marcus's hand.

As the final buzzer sounded, Georgetown University had pulled off the upset, claiming their place in history. Coach Thompson felt vindicated. He had always believed in his team, and now they stood as champions.

Meanwhile, back in the studio, Masterson and PHP faced the ultimate career-defining decision. Another multimillion-dollar record deal loomed, threatening to compromise their artistic integrity.

"I don't know, man," J-Dawg said, uncertainty in his voice. "This is everything we've dreamed of."

Dre nodded thoughtfully. "But at what cost? Are we willing to sacrifice our principles?"

FOR THE LOVE OF THE GAME

Masterson, silent for a moment, finally spoke. "We have to stay true to ourselves. We have to make music that means something."

J-Dawg and Dre exchanged glances. "But what if they don't want to hear it?" J-Dawg whispered.

"Then we walk away," Masterson said firmly. "We find another way."

They dove back into the music, pouring their hearts and souls into every beat and verse. Their sound was raw and unfiltered, a powerful statement of their values.

Now that the championship was in the rearview, Clifford was faced a life changing decision. His journalism career was taking off with national attention for his articles. A powerful editor offered him the opportunity of a lifetime.

"Clifford," the editor said. "We've been following your work. We think you have a gift for storytelling, and we want you to work for us and help shape national conversations. You have a unique skill and a power with words that are a natural born gift and cannot be taught in school. We want to harness that and touch the lives of the people."

Clifford's heart skipped a beat. But even as he basked in the offer, something held him back. "I love journalism, but I also love basketball too. I'm not ready to give that up."

The editor nodded. "You have a gift so don't let it go to waste. You can use it to make a difference. You can come on board after your career is over, and we will be here for you when you're ready. We spoke to coach Thompson, and he spoke very highly of you and having met you in person, I understand exactly what he meant when he described you to us."

As Clifford stepped back out into the city, he felt uncertain, but he knew he had a choice to make. One that would shape the trajectory of his future.

FOR THE LOVE OF THE GAME

Chapter 23: The Echoes of Glory

The Georgetown University Hoyas' locker room buzzed with pure joy. They had just toppled the Houston Cougars to claim their first national championship. Players and coaches celebrated, and the air was thick with the scent of sweat and triumph.

Malik sat in front of his locker, eyes closed, reflecting quietly. Named the tournament's Most Outstanding Player, he had transformed from raw talent into one of college basketball's most dominant forces. Yet, despite achieving his ultimate goal, unease lingered. What lay ahead for someone who had poured everything into one dream?

His brother Masterson's voice cut through the celebration. "Yo, Mal! You did it, man! You're a legend!"

Malik looked up to see Masterson, pride shining in his eyes, holding a bottle. "Thanks, Mass. But I couldn't have done it without everyone. This is a team victory."

C. GROOMS & BOBBY MAY

"I know, Mal. But you put this team on your back when it mattered most." Malik sighed. "But I don't know what's next. I've been chasing this dream for so long, and now that I've caught it, I feel like I'm standing on the edge of a cliff."

Masterson gripped his brother's shoulder. "Remember, this is just the beginning. You have an entire world of possibilities ahead. And no matter what, you'll always have your family and your brothers. Besides, word on the street is that you're going to be drafted in the first round of the draft."

"Where did you hear that?," Malik said with a puzzled look on his face. "Bro, for real? please don't tell me that you think folks don't see you balling out. Your games are nationally televised," Masterson burst out in an uncontrollable laughter. "Anyway, I hear things and unlike you, I'm not secluded under a rock not knowing that people see you." Malik just smiled at how observant his brother was and gave him a strong embrace.

FOR THE LOVE OF THE GAME

Across the room, Elijah embraced his mother and sister, their tears mingling. Despite the victory, unease gnawed at him. His father, a distant figure who had left years ago, lay in a hospital bed fighting for his life.

"Have you spoken with Dad? How is he? I feel like I have to visit him," Elijah whispered. "I have to be there, even if it's just to say goodbye."

His mother nodded. "We'll go together, as a family. I know that he gave you a tough time when you started playing basketball and it seemed like he was crushing your dream, but he wasn't. He was just afraid and was projecting his past failures and he didn't want to get his hops up high. He was following you this season and I know he saw tonight's game. Anyway, let me know when you want to go. On another note, I can see that you have another family here that loves and supports you. I can see why y'all won the championship. Unity and perseverance go a long way in this world, and I am super proud of you." Elijah tried to hold back some more tears, but his mother's words always had a way of penetrating his soul because she came from a place of love. When all else has had shortcomings in his life every now and then, love and support from his mother wasn't one of them.

Clifford sat in a corner, happy but contemplating his future. He has been torn for a little while now between his love for basketball and his passion for journalism, but now the season was officially over.

"What do you think, Coach?" he asked, approaching Coach Thompson.

"We're National Champions son. I am ecstatic and couldn't be happier. You played your ass off out there and for that I'm proud to be your coach and mentor."

"Coach, I was talking about the job opportunity that I have with the Washington Post."

"Oh, ok. Clifford, I can't tell you what to do right now, but I need you to understand that you have a rare gift for storytelling. As much as I love having you on this

FOR THE LOVE OF THE GAME

team, I believe you can make an even bigger impact through your writing. I've also made a few phone calls on your behalf during the season, but I wanted to wait until the season was over. In any event, you can add National Champion to your resume! I will always be here for you, so you have my blessing if you need to devote more time to your journalism career. You are still going to have your scholarship."

Clifford nodded and looked at his coach. It was the kind of look a son would give his father, after he's received approval and earned respect by completing a rite of passage. Walking away from basketball and the brotherhood would be the hardest thing he'd ever had to do up to this point, but for right now he was enjoying being a National Champion.

Later that evening, Masterson met up with PHP in a small Atlanta studio. They huddled around a mixing board after having spent months pouring their hearts into their music.

"This is it," Masterson said. "This is the album we were meant to make."

J-Dawg nodded. "It's a masterpiece."

Dre asked, "But what about the label? What about the fame and money?"

"We don't need them," Masterson replied. "We need our music and our integrity. If the world isn't ready, that's their loss."

And so, PHP set out on a new path, playing small clubs and building a loyal following. Critics praised their raw lyrics and genre-bending sound. Record labels came calling, but PHP remained true to themselves, ready to weather any storm together.

A few days later back on campus, Malik, Elijah, and Clifford began reflecting on their journey. They had faced challenges and triumphs that most could only dream of.

FOR THE LOVE OF THE GAME

"I couldn't have done this without you guys," Malik said. "You've been my rock."

Elijah nodded. "We're brothers, now and forever."

Clifford smiled. "Basketball was just the beginning of a journey that will last a lifetime."

As the sun set, casting a warm glow over the city, they knew they were ready for whatever came next. They had each other and the lessons they had learned. And with that knowledge burning bright in their hearts, they stepped out into the world, ready to embrace the future. The echoes of their glory would linger on long after the cheers had faded. Their story of brotherhood, perseverance, and unbreakable bonds will write the next chapter of their lives together.

C. GROOMS & BOBBY MAY

Chapter 24: The Road Ahead

The bustling energy of Jimmy Smalls' Above the Rim Basketball Tournament pulsated through Binghamton, New York. The city teemed with visitors, its streets alive with the thrill of competition and camaraderie. Amidst this vibrant atmosphere, a more complex narrative was unfolding on the town's outskirts.

Frank White, Jimmy's grandfather, presided over a modest empire along a two-mile strip off the highway. His domain included a gas station, waste management company, car repair shop, diner, and a 20-room motel. Once, the nearby Ravenswood Hotel & Suites had been the go-to destination for tournament visitors. However, the recent emergence of a casino haven, flanked by 20 new hotels, had diverted much of its clientele.

Frank, ever the shrewd businessman, had concocted a plan to boost his enterprise during tournament weekends. He discreetly manufactured road

FOR THE LOVE OF THE GAME

hazards, causing flat tires and minor fender benders. This ensured a steady stream of travelers needing repairs, meals, and lodging, all conveniently provided by Frank's businesses. To maintain the illusion of legitimacy, Frank kept four cars in his shop, two on lifts, giving the appearance of high traffic.

As the tournament reached its zenith, Jimmy decided to pay his family a visit. He missed his grandfather's gruff but loving presence and wanted to check on the family business. Little did he know, his visit would set in motion a chain of events that would change everything he thought he knew about his family's legacy.

That same evening, Masterson and three members of PHP were driving through the area, on their way to a show scheduled for the following night. The quiet of their journey was shattered by a sudden lurch of their SUV and a loud bang that echoed through the night.

"Damn, what now?" Masterson groaned, stepping out to inspect the damage.

C. GROOMS & BOBBY MAY

J-Dawg, ever practical, was already on his phone. "We need a tow. The closest repair shop is just down the road."

"Of course this happens now," Masterson muttered. "Perfect timing."

They carefully maneuvered their vehicle to White's Car Repair Shop, where they were greeted by Frank's friendly smile and assurances of quick service. Opting to stay at the nearby motel, the group found themselves at the diner, where Jimmy sat nursing a cup of coffee.

Recognition flashed in Jimmy's eyes. "Hey, aren't you Masterson from PHP?"

A conversation ensued, marked by the easy camaraderie of strangers brought together by circumstance. As they chatted, Jimmy couldn't shake the growing unease. The coincidence felt too convenient, stirring memories of his grandfather's "clever" business tactics.

FOR THE LOVE OF THE GAME

The next morning, Jimmy confronted Frank at the repair shop. Their exchange was tense, loaded with unspoken accusations and defenses.

"Grandpa, we need to talk," Jimmy began, his voice steady despite his inner turmoil.

Frank's eyes narrowed, sensing the shift in his grandson's demeanor. "What's on your mind, Jimmy?"

"I was talking to someone last night. They got a flat tire on the way here. Seems like a lot of people have car trouble around this time of year," Jimmy said, watching Frank's reaction closely.

Frank's eyes narrowed slightly, but he kept his tone light. "Well, it's a busy time. Lots of folks on the road, more chances for accidents."
"Yeah, but it seems like an awful lot of accidents," Jimmy pressed.

C. GROOMS & BOBBY MAY

Frank sighed, setting down his tools. "Alright, Jimmy, you got me. I might've encouraged a few mishaps here and there. But it's for the good of the business. Keeps people here, spending money at our places."

Jimmy's disappointment was evident. "Grandpa, that's dangerous! What if someone got hurt?"

"I've been careful," Frank defended, his voice firm but tinged with doubt. "No one's gotten hurt. It helps keep the money flowing in. You know how tough it's been since those new hotels and the casino opened up."

Their conversation ended in an uneasy truce, with Frank promising to reconsider his tactics. But Jimmy knew the promises weren't enough, and he needed to act.

Meanwhile, after the car was repaired, Masterson and PHP were preparing to leave town. But Masterson couldn't shake the feeling that something wasn't right. He decided to dig deeper, his investigative instincts kicking in.

FOR THE LOVE OF THE GAME

"Something weird happened today," Masterson told the group. "I think that repair shop is up to something."

"What do you mean?" J-Dawg asked, frowning.

"Just a feeling. Too many coincidences," Masterson explained.

"Yeah, but our car's fixed now. Let's just focus on the show," another member said.

Masterson nodded, but he couldn't shake the lingering doubts.

Over the next few weeks, Jimmy worked tirelessly to find legitimate ways to attract visitors to his family's businesses. He organized special events at the diner and motel, offering discounts and promotions during tournament weekends. He also collaborated with local businesses to create a network of services that would benefit the community and attract more tourists.

C. GROOMS & BOBBY MAY

Jimmy's efforts began to pay off. More people started visiting the diner and staying at the motel, drawn by the new promotions and events. The car repair shop still saw steady business, but without the need for manufactured road hazards. Frank watched his grandson's progress with a mix of pride and relief.

Masterson, intrigued by the strange coincidences of their Binghamton pit stop, conducted his own research. What he uncovered confirmed his suspicions: an unusually high number of minor accidents on that stretch of highway, all leading to Frank's repair shop.

Determined to uncover the truth, Masterson reached out to Jimmy. "I think your grandfather might have been causing those accidents on purpose," Masterson said over the phone.

Jimmy was silent for a moment, then sighed. "I had my suspicions too, so I confronted him with it, and he denied doing anything. Anyway, I need to be sure, so

FOR THE LOVE OF THE GAME

I set up some marketing and promotion to try and bring legit traffic to the area."

"Maybe we can work together," Masterson suggested. "Make sure he keeps his promise and finds better ways to boost the business."

"Yeah, I think that would be a good idea," Jimmy agreed. "I'm all for trying to do things the right way when it comes to business."

Together, they devised a plan to monitor the highway and ensure no more road hazards were being created. But they didn't stop there. Combining Jimmy's local knowledge with Masterson's entertainment connections, they brainstormed innovative ways to attract more visitors to Binghamton and Frank's businesses.

With Masterson's help, Jimmy organized a series of concerts and events at the motel and the diner featuring local bands and artists. These events drew large crowds and brought new business to the area.

C. GROOMS & BOBBY MAY

The community began to thrive, and Frank's businesses saw a new steady increase in legitimate revenue.

As the weeks passed, Jimmy and Masterson's friendship deepened. They bonded over their shared vision of making Binghamton a better place for everyone. Frank, witnessing the positive changes and his grandson's growth, felt a mix of pride and regret.

One evening, Jimmy and Masterson sat in the diner, enjoying a meal after a successful event and Frank joined them. His words were few but heartfelt.

"You boys have done a great job. I never would have thought of all these innovative ideas. When you live to be my age, there will be plenty of things that you look back on, and wish could've been done differently. The power of hindsight can be a gift and a curse. On one hand, you can look back and see the errors in your ways and implement changes going forward with the time that you have left on this Earth. The other side of the equation is even more telling; you could look back and know you messed up but not even care because it already happened. Don't take things for granted. When you know better, you do better."

The wise words of our elders should never go unnoticed because many have walked the path of trial and error in order to deliver knowledge to those who need it. Jimmy's response was simple but powerful. "I just wanted to make things better for you. I have to take some accountability too because in my mind, I thought everything was okay with your business. I turned a blind and was only focused on myself and for that I truly apologize."

Frank slowly nodded, understanding the implicit forgiveness in his grandson's words.

Masterson, sensing the weight of the moment, added a smile and chimed in, "Well, we're just getting started with our plan and I look forward to seeing things through. Where I come from, there aren't too many families that can build a legacy and even fewer that can sustain it for multiple generations. For a long time, I thought making money would provide me with solace and fulfillment. This couldn't be further from the truth. I understand the importance of money in the world that we live in, but I will take health and a peace of mind if I had to part with money. But hey enough about me, I'm ready to help create something that can benefit us all through the power of collaboration."

In the months that followed, Binghamton's reputation as a destination for tourists and visitors grew. The Above the Rim Basketball Tournament continued to draw large crowds, but now it was just one of many attractions. Frank's businesses thrived without the need for underhanded tactics, a testament to the power of innovation and integrity.

Jimmy and Masterson's partnership extended beyond Binghamton too as they worked to bring new events and opportunities in Pennsylvania, Texas, Ohio, and California.

FOR THE LOVE OF THE GAME

As for Frank, he found a new sense of purpose in supporting Jimmy and Masterson's endeavors. He ran his business with a renewed commitment to honesty and integrity, and he was proud of the positive impact they made in the area.

The transformation of Binghamton was more than just an economic revitalization. It was a story of redemption and of a community coming together to create a better future and culture. The hidden hazards that once plagued the town's roads had been replaced by opportunities, proving that with vision, determination, and a little help from the unexpected, even the most entrenched problems could be overcome.

As the sun set on another busy day in Binghamton, Jimmy and Masterson stood outside the revamped diner and watched visitors and locals alike enjoying the vibrant atmosphere they had helped create. The success of their venture had far-reaching implications. Not only had they revitalized Binghamton's economy, but they had also created a model for sustainable, community-focused development. Other small towns began to take notice, reaching out to Jimmy and Masterson for advice on how to rejuvenate their own communities.

Frank, once the orchestrator of deception, now became an advocate for ethical business practices. He shared his story with other business owners, warning them of the long-term consequences of shortcuts and dishonesty. His transformation became a powerful testament to the possibility of change, no matter one's age or past mistakes.

As for PHP, their unexpected detour in Binghamton had sparked a new direction in their music. Inspired by the town's transformation, they began to write songs that spoke of community, redemption, and the power of positive change. Their next album, partly recorded in Binghamton, became their most critically acclaimed work yet, resonating with audiences far beyond their usual fan base.

FOR THE LOVE OF THE GAME

The Above the Rim Basketball Tournament, once the sole draw to Binghamton, evolved into a multi-faceted cultural event. Jimmy and Masterson incorporated music performances, art exhibitions, and community workshops into the program, turning it into a celebration of local talent and creativity.

As word of Binghamton's renaissance spread, it caught the attention of national media. Journalists and filmmakers descended on the town, eager to document its remarkable turnaround. Jimmy and Masterson found themselves at the center of a whirlwind of interviews and feature stories, using their platform to spread their message of community-driven change.

The story of Binghamton's transformation even made its way into university curricula, becoming a case study in ethical business practices and community development. Students from across the country visited the town, eager to learn from its example. Well, except for the rigging of the roads.

C. GROOMS & BOBBY MAY

Jimmy and Masterson were sitting and talking late one night, reminiscing about the journey that brought them to this point. The once struggling establishment was now buzzing with life even at late hours.

"You know," Jimmy said, looking around at the diverse crowd of locals and visitors, "I never imagined we could make this much of a difference."

Masterson nodded, a thoughtful expression on his face. "It just goes to show what can happen when people come together with a common purpose. We didn't just change Binghamton; we changed ourselves and the culture for its local residents. I've been doing a lot of thinking about Frank's Diner and a possible expansion if you're open to the idea. Back home in NYC, there is a small neighborhood spot in Brooklyn on Washington Avenue called Tom's Diner. I would travel down from Harlem by subway just to go in there and experience the vibe. The place was a throwback to me. The cook knew everybody that came to the place by name, and he even knew what they liked to eat too. The place was small but felt much bigger and I'm probably understating the economic impact that it had on the local community. Anyway, I would like to create a franchise opportunity for Frank's. There's some paperwork that has to be done at the state level, but we can reach out to an associate of mine to make that happen if you like."

They continued their conversation well after midnight and mapped out a plan for the immediate future. Jimmy was intrigued by the idea as he thought about all of the successful franchises that ultimately had to start just like they did. "Masterson, even Mc Donald's, Burger King, and Golden Crust had to start somewhere. It's a great idea and I say let's do it."

Franchising is the culmination of real estate, innovation, and the power of entrepreneurship merging into a brand identity. Frank White's Diner was on its way.

Chapter 25: The Paths We Choose

Elijah sat in his Georgetown University dorm room, the textbook before him forgotten as his mind wandered. The sudden buzz of his phone shattered the silence, Marcus' name flashing on the screen. An uneasy feeling settled in his stomach as he answered.

"Elijah, Darius got shot and he's in critical condition." Marcus' voice trembled, heavy with emotion.

The words hit Elijah like a physical blow, knocking the air from his lungs. "What? What happened?"

"I don't know all the details, but it's bad man. He's in the ICU. He might not make it. Damn E, I know we've all been through our ups and downs, but I wanted you to know because at one time he was your brother."

Elijah's world spun as memories of Darius flooded his mind. They had been inseparable once, spending countless hours on the basketball court, perfecting

FOR THE LOVE OF THE GAME

their jump shots, and dreaming of a brighter future. But everything changed when Darius started down a different path.

"I can't believe this," Elijah whispered, his voice barely audible. "We used to be so tight. But then he got mixed up with the wrong crowd and everything just fell apart. Fuck!"

Marcus sighed heavily. "Yeah, I remember. It all started with those envelopes that he was dropping off for that guy in the neighborhood."

Elijah's mind flashed back to that fateful day, the moment that had driven a wedge between him and his once inseparable friend. Darius had been given a thick yellow envelope to deliver and when he returned, he had a smaller envelope stuffed with $5,000 in cash. It was more money than either of them had ever seen, and it had been the beginning of the end. The allure of cash is hard to turn down when you're young and have little in life. Materialism tends to do that to the youth who often succumb to it

C. GROOMS & BOBBY MAY

because the greater society puts so much value on it. Most times in Urban America, cash is not even a commodity for growth, it is a depreciating asset. Picture the irony of an asset depreciating, a true oxymoron.

"It was supposed to be just a one-time thing," Elijah said, his voice tinged with regret. "But then he kept doing it and chasing that easy money. He got in too deep and over his head and he couldn't even see it."

A heavy silence came between them.

"I tried to warn him," Marcus finally said. "Tried to tell him that nothing good could come from getting mixed up with those guys. But he wouldn't listen."

Guilt washed over Elijah as he remembered how he had watched Darius drift away, too focused on his own dreams to see the danger his friend was in. "I should have done more, Marcus. I should have tried harder to keep him away from that life."

FOR THE LOVE OF THE GAME

"Don't put that on yourself, Elijah. Darius made his own choices, just like we all did. You can't blame yourself for what happened."

But Elijah couldn't shake the feeling that he had let his friend down, that he had been too caught up in chasing his own dreams to see the struggles Darius was facing.

"I just never thought it would end like this," he said, his voice cracking. "Darius had so much potential, so much talent. And now, because of some stupid choices, it's all gone."

Marcus was quiet for a moment, the sounds of the city filtering through the phone. "I know, man. It's not fair. But we have to keep going, you know? We have to make something of ourselves, to show the world that we're more than just statistics."

Elijah knew Marcus was right, but the weight of Darius' situation felt like a physical burden pressing down on his chest and making it hard to breathe.

C. GROOMS & BOBBY MAY

"I just wish I could have done something, Marcus. I wish I could have saved him is all I'm saying."

"You can't save everyone, Elijah. But you can honor his memory by being the best version of yourself and by chasing your dreams and making something of your life."

A spark of determination ignited within Elijah, a fire that had been dimmed by the news of Darius' shooting. He knew that he had to keep pushing forward and to make his dreams a reality, not just for himself, but for all those who had been lost along the way. Elijah, the future NBA first round pick, had to sit back and analyze how even the smallest choices on any particular day can lead to larger decisions later on. Some people believe in fate and others embark on destiny, and sometimes the thin line between both comes down to our choices.

"You're right, Marcus. I can't let this break me. I have to keep going for myself, Darius and for everyone else who had limited opportunities. Some days it does

FOR THE LOVE OF THE GAME

feel like my back is against the wall and me against the world."

"That's the spirit, man. And you know I'm always here for you, right? No matter what happens, we've got each other's backs."

Elijah smiled, feeling a rush of gratitude for his friend. "I know, Marcus. And I'm here for you too. Always."

As they ended the call, Elijah leaned back in his chair, his mind racing with memories of Darius and the life they had once shared. He thought back to those early days when basketball was their only focus and the future seemed bright with possibility. But then came the money, the allure of fast cash and comfortable living. Darius had been seduced by the promise of wealth and power, and it had led him down a path of no return.

Elijah felt the tears coming again, but this time he let them fall. He made his way to the campus basketball court, the familiar feel of the ball in his hands offering a small comfort. He played for hours, each shot, each dribble a tribute to Darius, to the friendship they had once shared and the future they had dreamed of.

He played until his lungs burned, his legs ached, and until the sun began to set and long shadows stretched across the court. When he finally stopped, his heart was racing, and he was exhausted. Elijah decided to honor the memory of his friend who had a good heart but fell victim to the glitz and glamour of the street life. One thing about the streets is that they claim more lives than they save and they don't love anybody. The best thing we can do is learn how to navigate them.

As Elijah walked back to his dorm, his steps were heavy, but his spirit was slightly lifted. He knew that the road ahead would be tough and filled with obstacles to overcome. There were surely more losses to bear but coming from his circumstances had somewhat prepared him to push through the adversity. However, the loss of Darius showed just how short life was. If he wanted to make a mark on the world and give back to the community that had shaped him, then that would need to begin right now. Darius had introduced the love of the game to him so what happened? That was an answer that would never come but he vowed to never forget where he came from. A lot of dreams get shattered in our neighborhoods but there are too many that don't find what they love.

Even the most optimistic of people know that It's an arduous task to escape the multitude of traps specifically waiting for you. Love has a powerful effect on the brain and can have a variety of outcomes based on your own unique circumstances. Some people love the fame, others love the money, many love the fast life, and the love for the streets can give you all three. Sometimes to escape all of that, people like Elijah have to find the love of the game for basketball and hold on to the solace that it can provide.

Back in his room, Elijah pulled out his phone and called Marcus again.

"Hey, Marcus. It's Elijah. I was just thinking about Darius and everything that's happened. I just wanted to say thank you for being there for me and for understanding what I'm going through."

Marcus' voice was warm and comforting. "Of course, man. That's what friends are for. And I know how much Darius meant to you and how close you two were before everything went down."

Elijah felt a lump forming in his throat, his eyes stinging with unshed tears. "I just keep thinking about that day when he showed up with that envelope full of money. I could have done something. Maybe I should have tried harder to stop him. Damn, I can't do anything about the past, but I'm definitely going to do something for our community in the future. We are losing way too many people to the streets for real."

"Elijah, just remember that no matter what you did or didn't do differently that Darius had his own path, and you have yours. We can always learn from each other along the way and that is where our emotional intelligence and decision making come into play. Who are you when you think no one is looking at you?"

Elijah knew Marcus was right, but it didn't make the pain any easier to bear. "I just wish I could go back, you know?

"I know, man. But we can't change the past. All we can do is keep moving forward, keep fighting for a better future."

Elijah nodded, even though Marcus couldn't see him. "You're right. We have to keep pushing, for Darius and for everyone else who never got the chance to see their dreams come true."

"And we will, Elijah. We'll make it out of here and we'll make something of ourselves.

As they ended the call, Elijah felt a sense of peace settling over him. He knew that the pain of losing Darius would never fully go away, that there would always be a hole in his heart where his friend had once been. But he also knew that he had the strength and the support to keep going, to chase his dreams and to make a difference in the world. He had to do it for the love of the game.

FOR THE LOVE OF THE GAME

Chapter 26; Family & Loyalty

As the first light of morning gently embraced D.C., Malik found himself perched on the edge of his bed awake. His mind was abuzz with thoughts about the road and the obstacles awaiting him.

In a few weeks he would bid farewell to his home to chase his NBA dreams. The upcoming draft loomed large with every step and decision under scrutiny from scouts, coaches, and fans. Malik had given up everything for this opportunity to put his skills on display on basketball's biggest stage.

Yet in the hush of his room doubts crept in. The past year had rattled his confidence on a different level. He was forced to confront truths beyond the basketball court; from the Georgetown University scandal to his teammates struggles and the weight of his ambitions.

A gentle knock on the door broke through his contemplation. "Come in " he called out groggily.

C. GROOMS & BOBBY MAY

Elijah entered quietly, "What's up brother? I haven't talked to you in a couple of days, so I was just checking in on you."

Malik let out a sigh and rubbed his scalp. "I've been thinking a lot about what's to come E. Trying to figure out how to manage it all."

Elijah gave a nod, his understanding evident in his gaze. "I get it. It's a lot to take in. Just remember, you're not in this alone. You've got me, Clifford, and your family by your side. We're all here to support you."

Malik felt a lump forming in his throat as he absorbed Elijahs words. He knew it was the truth, but it still felt overwhelming.

"I just don't want to disappoint y'all I guess. There's a lot of things going through my mind and I'm just trying to work it out.

FOR THE LOVE OF THE GAME

Elijah placed a hand on Malik's shoulder. "You could never let us down. Your strength and resilience speak for themselves. No matter how things unfold, that won't change." Gratitude washed over Malik as he nodded in acknowledgment of Elijahs words. He got up from his seat ready to tackle the challenges of the day.

Meanwhile across town, Clifford was sitting in his office at The Washington Post. He embraced his opportunity as a writer and approached all of his assignments with unmatched vigor and enthusiasm with a goal of making an impact. A gentle knock on his office door broke his concentration momentarily.

"Come on in " Clifford called out. David Shapiro, the head editor walked in with a grin.

"Hey Clifford, how's it going?"

Clifford's face lit up. "I'm doing great sir. This position is everything I thought it would be and then some."

C. GROOMS & BOBBY MAY

David nodded, a look of approval shining in his eyes. "You definitely have the gift for storytelling and I'm confident you'll achieve great things here."

Clifford felt a surge of pride. "Thank you, sir. I won't let you down." Davids's smile grew wider. "I know you won't. I'll be here to support you every step of the way." David left the office and Clifford continued on with his project.

Elijah was deep in thought about his situation and was trying to process it. He had a great season and NBA scouts had taken notice, but he kept asking himself, 'Am I making the right choice?" His family made sacrifices that paved the way for him to be where he is right now. Even if he were to get drafted, could he truly repay his family for all that they had done so he could a chase a dream? It was a lot to consider. Malik knocked on the door, "E what's up brother? I'm heading out to the gym to put some shots up and clear my mind a little too. Are you coming through?" Elijah let out a sigh and opened the door, "I've been doing a lot of thinking about what lies

FOR THE LOVE OF THE GAME

ahead and wondering if basketball is truly the path that is meant for me. Three years ago, the answer would've been yes but today I'm not so sure. Don't get me wrong, the allure of making NBA money can't be undervalued or overlooked but chasing that dream was not the end all be all. You feel me?"

Malik nodded in understanding, his eyes reflecting empathy. "I understand where you're coming from. Your value in life extends beyond your skills on the basketball court and making the NBA wasn't the end goal of your dream. You want to do something else, but basketball was just your vehicle to get here." Malik paused and shifted the conversation, Yo E listen, I feel you bro. I do. I came over here to get you and see if you want to get some shots up. You have to keep your head clear, and this is how I do it, so I want you to join me."

A sense of calm washed over Elijah, "Yes, I'll go to the gym with you and thanks for listening brother. I barely let you get two feet in the door, and I bombarded you with my deep thoughts."

C. GROOMS & BOBBY MAY

Malik chimed in, "E, whatever it is that you want to do just let me know and I got you bro. I'm dead serious man. You're a good brother with a genuine heart and when I start stacking these NBA checks, I'm putting some money to the side specifically for you. I mean that too. So with that being said, can we get to the gym before you unload again?" They both burst into laughter and the world seemed okay again.

The passing of days turned into weeks and months, and the trio pursued their aspirations while staying connected. Malik immersed himself in draft preparations dedicating his time to training sessions and meetings with agents and scouts. Clifford pursued his passion for storytelling by seeing his name frequently in the pages of the Post. Meanwhile, Elijah carved his path by balancing his passion for law with a commitment to supporting his family.

Their bond remained resilient throughout it all too. They celebrated each other's triumphs and provided solace during challenging moments which always helped in lifting their collective spirits up. Late night

FOR THE LOVE OF THE GAME

calls and text exchanges helped them stay connected even as their paths began to diverge. One evening as Malik sat reviewing scouting reports in his apartment, a message from Elijah lit up his phone.

"Just wanted to let you know I'm proud of you bro."
"You're living the dream we all shared once. Remember your roots but don't let them hold you back " Malik was touched as he typed his response.

"I wouldn't be here, without you and Cliff. You guys are my support system. Wherever life takes me you'll always be my brothers " he added gratefully.

Clifford was burning the midnight oil at the Post pouring his heart into a story that he hoped would create an impact. His phone buzzed with a message from Malik.

"I read your article brother. You're making waves buddy. Keep speaking truth to power."

Clifford's face lit up with motivation as he replied.

C. GROOMS & BOBBY MAY

"Thanks, Mal. Your encouragement means the world to me. Bro, I'm excited to see you going to the league. Hope all is well with the family."

The trio found time to reunite at their cherished spot near campus where they had spent countless times together. Reflecting on their journey, Elijah marveled,

"Look at where we are now. A rising star in the NBA, a journalist, and a future lawyer."

Clifford chimed in quickly, "Wait, what? You're going to Law School? Wow. That's so dope brother. Ironically, I could actually see you doing that. I'm proud of you."

Elijah opened up, "I was having a great season during our championship run but something was always eating away at me and then, my guy from back home, Darius died. His death hit home for real, and it was a wakeup call on how short life can be. When we were coming up in Camden things got beyond rough when the city implemented a law that imposed a curfew in

FOR THE LOVE OF THE GAME

most of the parks from 9pm to 7am. The restaurants in the area had to shut down too between the hours of 11pm to 7am. In essence, they were trying to eliminate the night life, as if that had anything to do with what was going on during the day. I used to work out in the evenings after 9 and then just like that, it was gone. It forced me to change my schedule, and my eyes opened up to the decay and drugs that flooded my community. There was crime too, a lot of it, and even if I wasn't seeing it, it was there. My passion for law began there when I was directly impacted by the decisions of other people. I'm going to the Georgetown School of Law program."

Malik flashed a smile as he draped an arm around Elijahs shoulders, "We're just scratching the surface and there is a lot that we can accomplish. All we have to do is put our minds together. Elijah, do you remember what I told you a few months back? I got your back no matter what and I already started putting money aside."

Clifford chimed in with a nod of approval and a slogan, Elijah Williamson, Esq, a man of the people and for the republic for which it stands." They laughed at the idea, but they could see it come to fruition. Amidst their laughter and banter, the bittersweet reality of their separation lingered in the air. There was also an undercurrent of excitement for the adventures that awaited them.

"Here's something I need from y'all", Malik said earnestly. "No matter where life leads us or how hectic things get lets always carve out time for one another. We're family so that bond needs to remain unbreakable."

Elijah and Clifford both nodded in agreement.

"Family" echoed Elijah.

"Forever" added Clifford.

As the evening progressed, they mapped out gatherings like cheering on Malik during his games,

FOR THE LOVE OF THE GAME

brainstorming ideas for Clifford's articles, and providing support as Elijah pursued his studies. They found solace in their unity and their bond was strengthened by the shared trials they had faced. It transcended beyond basketball or journalism; it was about the journey they had embraced, the relationship that they had built, and the unwavering faith they held in each other's abilities.

As they bid farewell that evening, each venturing back to their paths, a mix of emotions lingered. An old chapter was closing while a fresh one awaited. Despite whatever adversities awaited them in the future they were prepared to confront them as a front, bound by their intertwined history and aspirations for what lie ahead.

The tale of Malik, Elijah and Clifford extended beyond sports or camaraderie. It embodied the endurance of resilience, the strength of affection and allegiance, and the enduring bonds of brotherhood. Stepping into this phase of their lives, they carried with them the wisdom and reminiscences from their shared experiences as they poised to leave an impact on society.

FOR THE LOVE OF THE GAME

Chapter 27: Survival of the Fittest

The atmosphere was electric at the Bethel High School gymnasium in Hampton, Virginia. Chuck Jackson, a two-sport All-American athlete, sank his final shot. The scoreboard flashed an impressive 50 points, sealing a thrilling victory. Riding high on adrenaline, Chuck and five of his teammates decided to extend their celebration to the Circle Lanes Bowling Alley.

Unbeknownst to Chuck, Clifford had traveled to Hampton for the weekend at the request of a friend. She urged him to watch Chuck play and potentially write a feature story about the rising star. Clifford, awestruck by Chuck's performance, made a mental note to catch up with him later at the bowling alley.

As the night progressed at Circle Lanes, the initial celebratory vibe among Chuck and his friends began to shift. An undercurrent of racial tension permeated the air, growing thicker with each passing moment. Clifford, sensing the changing dynamics, decided to leave at 11 p.m., just as the atmosphere began to feel uncomfortably charged.

At 11:30 p.m., the simmering tension erupted. A simple accident at the snack bar, a spilled tray of food, ignited a racially charged brawl between black and white patrons. The once jovial bowling alley transformed into a chaotic battleground.

During the mayhem, one of Chuck's quick-thinking friends recognized the potential consequences for the high-profile athlete. Without hesitation, he whisked Chuck away from the scene, driving him to safety at a friend's house. By midnight, they arrived at their destination. Coincidentally it was the same house where Clifford was staying for the weekend.

Chuck paced the living room; his mind replaying the night's events on a loop. His body remained tense with adrenaline still coursing through his veins. The creak of the door announced Clifford's entrance, concern etched on his face.

FOR THE LOVE OF THE GAME

"Chuck, I'm Clifford Michaels," he began, his voice calm but tinged with worry. "I saw your game earlier and was at the bowling alley about an hour ago. I just heard what went down. Are you all right?"

Chuck took a deep breath before responding. "Yeah, I'm alright. It's just, I can't believe what just happened. One minute we were having fun, and the next, chairs were flying. I barely got out of there."

Clifford nodded, understanding the weight of the situation. "That's crazy, man. I'm glad you're safe. I came down here to write a story about you. Your 50-point game tonight was incredible! You've got serious talent, Chuck. I can see you making it to the league without a doubt."

Despite the chaos of the night, Chuck listened intently to Clifford's words. "Thanks, C. I appreciate that. But right now, all I can think about is what happened back there. It was like everything just exploded."

C. GROOMS & BOBBY MAY

Clifford leaned forward with a serious expression serious. "I get it, man. But you can't let this mess get in your head. You've got a gift, and you need to keep pushing forward. Think about your future, think about the NBA."

Chuck sat down, rubbing his temples. The images of the brawl kept flashing through his mind. "I hear you. It's just, it's not just about basketball anymore. It's about everything else that comes with it. The expectations, the pressure, and now this. The racial tension down here is crazy. I've dealt with it my whole life pretty much but tonight was on another level. Where are you from Clifford?"

"Canton, Ohio. My family is from the Lathrop section of Canton, and they experienced extreme systemic racism because of redlining practices. Thousands of people were displaced when the city decided to run a highway through their neighborhood. Even to this day, the revitalization projects that take place throughout the state rarely hit my neighborhood. The racism was more systemic than direct, but I understand where you're coming from. My neighborhood was labeled as 'on the decline' and was effectively redlined. We had scarce resources to say the least. I grew up in poverty and although people associate Canton with the NFL Hall of Fame, there was very few historic things left during my childhood."

Clifford's voice was still firm and encouraging but filled with empathy. "Chuck, you're going to face a lot of challenges on and off the court. But you've got the talent and the heart to overcome them. Don't let tonight define you. This isn't just a small distraction and yes, it's a serious situation. But in the end, you come out as a winner. I know that Coach Thompson always has room for a player with heart, talent, and grit. Georgetown University would love to have you."

Chuck looked up, meeting Clifford's gaze. He saw sincerity and determination there, and it sparked a glimmer of hope within him.

"Thanks, C. I needed that. I won't let them get to me. I'm going to stay focused on my dreams and keep my composure. Man, this was absolutely a crazy situation."

As the night wore on, Chuck felt the tension slowly beginning to ease. Surrounded by supportive friends and Clifford's encouraging words, he knew he had the strength to endure. However, he also recognized that there would be more adversity ahead. The incident at the bowling alley was a stark reminder of the complex world he would have to navigate as he pursued his athletic dreams.

FOR THE LOVE OF THE GAME

Chapter 28: Reflections

In the last four years a lot had changed for Malik Wright, Elijah Williamson, and Clifford Michaels. They had all charted their paths to success in their fields while staying true to their origins.

Malik, now a star in the NBA with the New York Knicks, looked out at the city's skyline from his penthouse. His journey had been full of sacrifices and hurdles but every moment on the basketball court felt like it was all worth it. The city had embraced him, and he felt a sense of belonging both on and off the court.

Meanwhile in downtown Newark, New Jersey, Elijah had just launched his law firm. The sleek and modern office was a cry from the run-down buildings of his past. He has a Juris Doctor degree and bar certifications across many states including Ohio, New York, Maryland, Virginia, and New Jersey. Elijah had brought his vision to life and even though it was Malik's $25 million investment that kickstarted the venture, it was Elijahs unwavering dedication that steered the firm towards its mission of aiding underserved communities and areas.

As for Clifford, he had discovered his passion in the world of publishing. From his office, at Ascension Consulting & Publishing Services, Inc., he managed a group of magazines. The publications covered subjects including sports, entertainment, and social justice, enabling Clifford to share his compassionate stories.

The music group PHP, led by Masterson, sold 12 million albums in the last five years, and toured worldwide while staying true to their origins. They made a return to Binghamton for the AAU Tournament to honor their partnership with Jimmy Smalls, a major figure in the AAU world.

One evening with the sun setting behind the New York skyline, Clifford held a video conference with Elijah and Malik. The atmosphere was serious as he revealed news of a scandal affecting the basketball community. The U.S. Attorney General had launched an investigation into grassroots basketball and activities linked to the Above the Rim Tournament.

"We need to take action, and someone should let Masterson know about the scandal too." Clifford started urgently but calmly, "The families involved will require support."

"Elijah can one of your law offices help out?" Elijah agreed, brainstorming strategies, in his head. "I'm on it. I'll start gathering a team of our lawyers."

Malik leaned in with an expression. "Whatever resources you require, I'll make sure you have them. This goes beyond basketball and it's about safeguarding these kids and their futures. I'll contact Masterson and give him a heads up."

Meanwhile at a park, in Newark, New Jersey, 12-year-old Bellamy O'Neal practiced by himself. The rhythmic sound of the bouncing basketball reverberated through the evening air. A sleek SUV pulled up nearby and a local coach stepped out to approach Bellamy.

"What shoe size do you wear?" the coach inquired, eyeing the boys' worn-out sneakers.

Bellamy paused with the ball tucked under his arm. "Size eleven." he responded cautiously. The coach's grin widened as he spoke, "Okay great. I have your size, but I also have some plans in store for you. Just keep honing your skills because you definitely got what it takes." Watching the coach drive off in his SUV, Bellamy's eyes sparkled with a mix of hope and determination which reignited his aspirations.

Back in the city, Clifford, Elijah, and Malik understood that the scandal would cast a wide net over the whole basketball scene. They had experienced a similar situation while at Georgetown University, but this felt different. Nevertheless, they were prepared. Together they vowed to navigate through the madness to safeguard the dreams and futures of aspiring players like Bellamy O'Neal. As night fell upon the landscape,

FOR THE LOVE OF THE GAME

Malik looked out of his window with a sense of responsibility weighing on him. Elijah buried himself in his office making calls to rally his team for the battle that lay ahead. Clifford began crafting a piece aimed at unveiling the truth about systemic racism in sports, how the impoverished and underserved are affected, and for standing up for those in need.

The quest for justice had only just got started. With each passing day Malik, Elijah and Clifford felt closer to making an impact. However, the future remained uncertain, but their resolve was unwavering.

These are the efforts that help rising young stars find inspiration and garner support from others. Life often presents multiple truths simultaneously, but one undeniable constant remains; many folks will continue to risk it all For the Love of The Game.

C. GROOMS & BOBBY MAY

About The Authors

C. Grooms is a published author, educator, certified life coach, consultant, and podcaster who brings intellect, strategy, and lived experience to every space he enters. With academic training in Deviant Behavior and Social Control, Media and Communications, American Studies, and Sports Management, Grooms operates with both range and precision. His expertise allows him to speak to the realities of underserved communities, the pressure placed on young athletes, and the systemic gaps in education and leadership. He doesn't speculate — he educates, equips, and elevates.

As the co-founder of *The Two Grumpy Men*, he leads with clarity and conviction, building a platform that blends cultural storytelling with community impact. His writing is layered with insight and driven by purpose. His coaching and consulting are rooted in results. Whether in print, in person, or behind the mic, he is committed to delivering content that moves people forward.

He writes because the stories are real. He speaks because the message matters. He shows up because the next generation deserves more than recycled advice. They deserve the truth backed by proof.

FOR THE LOVE OF THE GAME

Bobby May spent over 20 years as a Catastrophe Claims Adjuster, helping individuals and families recover after some of life's most unexpected challenges. But his passion for serving others started long before that. His exceptional career began working as a staff member in group homes for juveniles. He saw firsthand the struggles many young people face without proper guidance and support. That experience inspired Bobby to open his own group homes, providing a safe space and structured environment for adolescents in need. Later, he worked as a Behavioral Specialist, helping youth navigate emotional and behavioral obstacles. These roles solidified his lifelong commitment to mentoring and uplifting the next generation.

Bobby May holds a Bachelor's degree in Criminal Justice with a concentration in Forensic Psychology and a Master's degree in Criminal Justice with an emphasis in Project Management. Today, he continues that mission through his work as a certified Life Coach, Business Consultant, and co-host of the Two Grumpy Men podcast, a platform where real talk meets life lessons and no topic is off-limits.

Whether Bobby is working with youth, coaching clients, or speaking from the mic, his goal remains the same: to help others unlock their potential, take control of their journey, and push forward no matter the obstacles. My motto is simple and personal: **Only the strong survive**. And true strength comes not just from what you've been through, but from what you're willing to rise above.

C. GROOMS & BOBBY MAY

Acknowledgements

Bobby May

First and foremost, I want to give a salute to my partner in crime, C. Grooms. We've been rocking for close to 40 years, and these ideas and plans started in college and on many road trips!!! LOL. Love you FAM!!!

I want to thank my family, especially my wife, for always believing in me, whether we're up or down. Love you for that always!! BK2NJ!!! Thank You to my beautiful daughters Chynna, NY-Jah, Kaya, and Breyla (BKNYC) for always holding daddy down and keeping me up on shit!! Lol. Special shout out to Mom Dukes because none of this would be possible without you!! You've been in my corner my whole life!!! You made me strong to get through any obstacle life threw at me, so Thank you, Mommy!!! Love you!! RIP to my Pops!!! The flyest OG!!! I wish you could be here to see this!!! LOL. RIP to my Grandparents, thank ya for instilling the best in me!!! Love ya!!

Shout to my sisters!!! Dionne, Diahann, and Monique!! Thank ya for loving your brother for who he is and for always reminding me that my name is Bobby!!! Special shout out to my brotha Big Dee, the "Infamous Ben Drake"!!! Who has been right there with me through thick and thin times!!! Love you, Fam!!! The only Drake I know!!! LOL

To all my people in Brooklyn, Staten Island (Park Hill building 141), Central Islip, NY, Baltimore, and Atlanta. Cannot forget my fam in Jamaica, Canada, and England. I can go on for days!! Love everyone who stayed down with our movement!!!! 1 Love

FOR THE LOVE OF THE GAME

C. Grooms

To my wife, **Natalie**, you are the anchor of our family and the calm in every storm. You've held me down with grace, lifted me with conviction, and reminded me who I am when the world tried to blur the picture. You are more than a partner; you are the queen of this legacy. Nothing I've built would stand the way it does without your unwavering presence, discernment, and belief in me.

To my children, **Stanley, Elaina, and Tsion**: you are my compass and my continuity. Every move I make is legacy-driven, and you are that legacy in motion.

To my **mother**, thank you for showing me what compassion looks like when it's rooted in strength. You were my first mirror and remain a blueprint for selfless love. To my brothers, **Darren, Craig, and Lamont**, you've walked with me through every season, solid and true.

To my **father, Stanley Grooms Jr.**, you sparked my early transformation. You didn't just guide me, you equipped me. You put sacred texts and sharp truths in my hands before most had even started asking questions. You gave me direction when it mattered most and continue to rest in peace.

To my extended family: my **aunts, uncles, nieces, nephews**, and their children, your presence has mattered more than you know. And especially to my cousins **Ronnie, Shieda, Valerie, Monique, Danny, and Monifa**, your love is loud, your loyalty unmatched.

C. GROOMS & BOBBY MAY

To my family at **John Jay College**, **Old Westbury**, and **Bishop Loughlin Memorial High School**, thank you for sharpening my thinking and refining my perspective.

To my **brothers from other mothers: A.B., T.O., Mike Lloyd, Santos, Booms, Barry G, and Bobby May,** our brotherhood is etched in authentic experiences. What we've built, protected, and stood for together speaks for itself. I absolutely love each and every one of you!

One love to **Sharia Marcus-Carter, Terez Mychelle, and Marjahna Segers,** three of the realest and kindest human beings I ever met. Each of you has a special place in my heart. You show me love no matter what and I appreciate each of you more than you know. To **East Harlem** and **Prospect Heights**, you gave me my edge, my rhythm, and my sense of code. You were my first classroom. There are literally way too many folks to name, but I must acknowledge the fallen generals Big P and my brother E.

To **Black Dot, Randy (ESSO) Parker**, the **Urban X family**, the **Bag Fuel Podcast**, and my **ESSO University fam**: you each represent a rare balance of insight, truth, and cultural currency. Thank you for always elevating the conversation. We are literally paving the road for the next generation of authors, visualists, content creators, clothing lines, photographers, and movie makers.

And to everyone not named but never forgotten, your impact lives in these pages.

Respect.

FOR THE LOVE OF THE GAME

https://fortheloveofthegame.xyz

C. GROOMS & BOBBY MAY

www.ingramcontent.com/pod-product-compliance
Lightning Source LLC
Chambersburg PA
CBHW071233080526
44587CB00013BA/1599